A Shell Guide

Derbyshire

Dedication: FRATRI DILECTISSIMO

A Shell Guide

Derbyshire

by Henry Thorold

Faber & Faber 3 Queen Square London

First published in 1972
by Faber and Faber Limited
3 Queen Square London WC 1
Printed in Great Britain by
Billing & Sons Limited, Guildford and London
All rights reserved

ISBN 0 571 08916 X

Illustrations

from AN ANCIENT RHYME

Respecting Welbeck Abbey, Hardwick Hall, Bolsover
Castle, and Worksop Manor—written about the year
1620, by a Dr Andrewes.

Hardwicke for hugeness, Worsope for height,
Welbecke for use, and Bolser for sighte;
Worsope for walk, Hardwicke for hall,
Welbecke for brewhouse, Bolser for all.
Welbecke a parish, Hardwicke a court,
Worsope a pallas, Bolser a fort;
Bolser to feast, Welbecke to ride in,
Hardwicke to thrive, and Worsope to hide in.
Hardwicke good house, Welbecke good keepinge,
Worsope good walkes, Bolser good sleepinge;
Worsope is wise, Welbecke is wittie,
Hardwicke is hard, Bolser is prettie;
Hardwicke is rich, Welbecke is fine,
Worsope is statelie, Bolser divine.

Acknowledgements

Christopher Hobhouse wrote the original *Shell Guide to Derbyshire* in 1935. I remember picking the book up in Spottiswoode's at Eton soon after it was published. It was the first *Shell Guide* I had ever seen. It thrilled me, and I became, what I have ever since been, an avid collector of *Shell Guides*.

So when in 1966 Sir John Betjeman kindly invited me to write another volume in the series, I immediately asked to do Derbyshire, not only for the admiration and affection which I have long felt for that county (next-door-but-one to my own), but also as an act of *pietas* to Christopher Hobhouse, and to the Editors of the *Shell Guides*.

Christopher Hobhouse's *Derbyshire* was out of print many years ago, and he himself was killed serving in the Royal Marines in 1940. His *Derbyshire* was brilliant, and much of his Introduction has been incorporated in the present Introduction. But his gazetteer was very brief indeed (as was the way with the earliest *Shell Guides*). So the Gazetteer is entirely of 1972, with the spice of an occasional quotation from Christopher Hobhouse.

I owe a great debt of gratitude to friends in Derbyshire and elsewhere. Sir John Every took me to thirteen great houses which are not normally open to the public. Mr Henry Jenney took me to places which I would never otherwise have seen, and entertained me on countless occasions at Ticknall. Canon Paul Miller was my guide in Derby itself. Mr Roger Evans introduced me to Matlock. Mr Jasper More, M.P., first opened my eyes to the important role played by the Midland Railway in Derbyshire, and helped me with much railway history. I also wish to express my gratitude to the following for their help: Mr Howard Colvin; Mr Mark Girouard; the Revd Claude Handford; the Revd Gerard Irvine; Miss Rosemary Irvine; Mr James Lees-Milne; Miss Rosemary Meynell; Sir Nikolaus Pevsner; Mr Reresby Sitwell; Mr H. J. Wain; Mr D. C. Wheadon; and the Revd T. B. Williams. I am also very grateful to all those who so kindly took me round their houses, or their churches, and often entertained me so generously.

I owe a special debt of gratitude to my cousin Lord Rossmore, who flew over from Ireland specially on several occasions to take photographs; to Mr Edward Piper for his photographs; finally to Mr John Piper, Editor of the *Shell Guides*, for untold help—with memories of much pleasurable hospitality at Fawley Bottom.

HENRY THOROLD

Marston Hall, Lincolnshire
January 1972

Introduction

HOW TO SEE DERBYSHIRE

Nine-tenths of Derbyshire is drained by a single river—the Trent. After passing through Burton, ten miles south of Derby, this health-giving river receives in turn the contributions of the Dove, the Derwent and the Erewash. These three rivers all flow practically due south into the Trent; their three valleys are the main natural lines of communication, and the high grounds between them form the main geological divisions. These divisions are four, and they are of the first importance, for they give to Derbyshire its four distinct types of landscape.

The first and southernmost district is the sandstone area south of a line from Derby itself to Ashbourne. It is a country of oak and thorn, of rust-coloured houses and rust-coloured fields, not especially distinguishable from any other parts of the Midlands, but containing some fine architecture and magnificent trees; this area is all low-lying, and is watered by the less picturesque stretches of the Dove, which, after emerging from its wonderful dale, becomes a broader and more complacent river, prone to floods and less hospitable to fish. It is also a country of power-stations. All along the valley of the Trent the

◁ Cresswell Crags
▽ Sutton Scarsdale

p10 Chee Dale ▷
p11 Dovedale

Between Chelmorton and Over Haddon

banks of this great river are now littered with these new monsters. There are five of them, either in Derbyshire, or within a stone's throw of the frontier. In themselves they are no doubt remarkable things: on a sunny day when their great cooling towers are standing white against a clear blue sky, or when great cascades of steam are pouring over their sides, they have perhaps a strange beauty of their own. But they change the scale of everything for miles around. They may fascinate, but they also overwhelm.

The second geological area comprises the coal-measures. Though coal is worked in widely scattered parts of Derbyshire, it is concentrated upon the valleys of the Erewash and the Rother. East of a line drawn from Derby to Chesterfield, all up the Nottinghamshire border, hardly a village is without its pit-head. Ilkeston, Clay Cross, North Wingfield, Normanton, Staveley,

Bolsover—it is like a goods train passing by. This is not generally regarded as holiday country—but it is irresistible country, especially for the amateur of architecture, and the appreciator of the unexpected. Some of the country's best buildings are here, standing noble, perhaps, in some pit-scarred valley, or lonely on some grimy hilltop—Hardwick, Bolsover, Sutton Scarsdale among the houses, Chesterfield, Sandiacre, Morley among the churches.

The third and central area runs from the valley of the Derwent to the valley of the Dove, and comprehends the great stretch of moorland that lies between. It is the limestone area, the Low Peak, or, if you prefer the name, the Wapentake of Wirksworth. Through limestone a river drives its channel deep, or even quite often under-

Chelmorton ▷

12

Two views near Beeley

ground. The Derwent valley is narrow, and at Matlock is little more than a gorge; but the Dove Valley from its source to Ashbourne is far narrower, and far too narrow, thank heaven, for a road. The Dove accordingly pursues its way in peace, while the Derby to Buxton road is forced to follow roughly in the tracks of the old Roman road, clean over the high ground. Extraordinary country it is, too—a country of ancient quarries and still more ancient mines, scattered over with

the remains of old superstition in barrows and lows and circles of stones, and sprinkled with bleak inhospitable villages, where immemorial customs and beliefs are dying harder than anywhere in Britain.

Finally there is the High Peak, the great barren area of gritstone that lies north of a line from Buxton to Chesterfield. This is the Derbyshire that one comes to see—the countryside itself—where London seems a thousand miles away. This is the land of loose stone walls, of vast areas of peat, of tors and edges and caverns and waterfalls. This is the paradise of the clau-

◁ Below The Peak near Glossop

15

Arbor Low

strophobe, where he can set an unlimited moor against an unlimited sky. This country is appreciated much, but it is a marvel that it is not appreciated more. "I can assure you," wrote Byron, "there are things in Derbyshire as noble as Greece or Switzerland." Why, one feels, motoring over the Snake Road, less than two hundred miles from London, why go further afield?

Start from Derby itself and follow the Derwent Valley to Rowsley, Bakewell or Baslow. From there make your excursions to Bolsover, and Hardwick in the extreme east, to Arbor Low, Stanton Moor, Youlgreave and Winster to the south, and to Chatsworth and Haddon close at hand. There also, if you are a fisherman, you must fish. Then make your preparations for the Peak. If the weather is bad, stay at Buxton; if it is fine, at Edale. Give a few days to the district bounded by Chapel, Hayfield, Glossop, Castleton and Tideswell. Do not, in any case, omit

Buxton, which has many charms of its own, apart from its convenience as a headquarters for the Peak. When you come away from Buxton, you must follow the Ashbourne road, at the same time making as many detours into Dovedale as you can, at Hartington, Lode Mill, and Thorpe. How much of Dovedale you will see depends on your powers of walking. If you can walk from Hartington to Thorpe, so much the better, for there is a path for the whole of that miraculous seven miles. In Dovedale again the fisherman will find himself delayed for an indefinite time. Arriving at Ashbourne, you can return to Derby either direct or round the south by Sudbury. Sudbury deserves an expedition, though the Dove has lost its charm beyond this point, and the country is characteristic Midland. So you will return to Derby, having seen in a week, or more probably a month, more wonderful country than you thought that England had.

ARCHITECTURE

But Derbyshire is not just beautiful countryside: it is a county rich in architecture. And it may perhaps come as a shock to a visitor, brought up on its legendary beauty, to discover that Derbyshire is very far from being an agricultural county. There is indeed arable land in the south; there is good pasture in the central limestone moorland, and coarse grazing in the High Peak. But Derbyshire is first and foremost an industrial county. Outside Dovedale, you will hardly get a glimpse of Derbyshire that does not embrace a viaduct, a furnace, a quarry, a mill, or a power-station. And none of these is necessarily ugly—indeed they can at times very easily be beautiful. The slick line of a slag heap is perhaps an acquired taste, as maybe is the sinister presence of a vast power-station—but everybody with an eye for form must love a railway cutting, and there can be no question about the charm of the discreetly busy little quarries and mill (some of the latter architectural marvels) which spring upon one round every corner of the limestone valleys. They have an air of immemorial usefulness. Let us then consider the buildings of Derbyshire.

The earliest of all must come first of all: the impressive stone circles. Arbor Low near Youlgreave, the Bull Ring at Dove Holes, the Nine Stones near Wheston, the Nine Ladies at Harthill and other stones on Stanton Moor—these all stand on high ground, and all within a few miles of each other. But they stand alone in history: none can be much later than 2000 B.C. Between them and the few fragments of the Roman occupation there is little.

And of these few Roman fragments there is little to see: remains of a large bath were dug up at Buxton (Aquae) in 1780, during the construction of the Crescent. There were the three Roman

forts of Derventio (Little Chester), Melandra (Glossop), and Anavio (Brough). There are still the Roman roads, the most important being Ryknield Street, which still runs straight as a die most of the way from Derby to Burton and Lichfield.

And then the churches: compared with the great churches of East Anglia or Somerset, they are not spectacular—but they are full of interest. Of early times there is the precious Saxon crypt of Repton—and many a Saxon cross, and the Saxon carved panel at Wirksworth. Melbourne is one of the grandest Norman churches in England, and Steetley, though small, one of the choicest. There are the Norman tympana, at Hognaston, at Parwich, at Ault Hucknall; there are Norman arcades and towers, such as those at Whitwell and Bradbourne. Of later churches, that at Ashbourne is memorable, as is Chesterfield—both big cruciform town churches. Tideswell is a complete building of the Decorated period. The chancels of Sandiacre and Norbury are superb for any county. There are spires of note at Breadsall and Ashbourne and Bonsall and of course at Chesterfield. Morley is glorious for its glass and its tombs.

p20 Tideswell▷
p21 Ashbourne Church

◁ Repton crypt
▽ Bradbourne

△ Cressbrook Mill
◁ Calver Mill

23

Of the seventeenth and eighteenth centuries Foremark church and the Willoughby chapel at Wilne, with its glass and its tiles, lonely and forgotten near the Trent, are Gothic Survival. Trusley and Mapleton are endearing little Georgian churches: James Gibbs' All Saints at Derby is a grand period building of the eighteenth century.

Characteristic of Derbyshire are the churches of the nineteenth century: many an industrial village or town has its Victorian (or earlier) church. Middleton-by-Wirksworth comes to mind, as do Handley, St George's New Mills, Calow, and Riddings. Not many are by famous architects: Gilbert Scott built Edensor, Butterfield Bamford. Many are the work of H. J. Stevens, the Derby architect. Later in the century are those by P. H. Currey. There is the Arts and Crafts church of St Andrew's, Langley Mill, and most beautiful of all, the little chapel of St John Baptist at Matlock, by Guy Dawber.

There are, too, three early Nonconformist churches of great interest: the Chinley Chapel (1667), the Elder Yard Unitarian Chapel at Chesterfield (1694), and the Moravian Chapel at Ockbrook (1750). Equally, the R.C. churches at Hassop (1816) and Glossop (1836), and St Mary's at Derby (by Pugin, 1838) are of note.

As for the towns, Ashbourne makes an instant appeal with its distinguished main street. There are grand town houses in Friargate, Derby. Buxton is a place of considerable individuality: John Carr's Crescent and Square are first-rate town architecture, while the spacious tree-lined roads of Victorian houses have something of the prosperous atmosphere of Eastbourne or North Oxford. Matlock, too, has charm and character. In quite a different way there is a grim attractiveness about Belper or Glossop with their mills and factories and terraces of early nineteenth century houses, or New Mills with its viaducts and decaying warehouses. Several villages call for special mention: Tissington for its setting, Snelston and Osmaston for their many pretty cottages, Sudbury for its handsome street, Edensor as a mid-nineteenth-century model village. Stone predominates in the north: brick in the south, where the gentler countryside merges with Leicestershire and Staffordshire.

But the influence of industry is never far away, and several early industrial buildings are of considerable importance—such as Arkwright's first mill at Cromford (1771), and the Masson Mill (1783) nearby, Calver Mill (1803) at Curbar, Strutt's North Mill at Belper (1804)—together with the vast later nineteenth-century mills nearby, and George Brettle's Warehouse with its dignified façade in Chapel Street—Walter Evans' early nineteenth-century Mill at Darley Abbey, and the many mills of the 1840s at Glossop. Most beautiful of all is the Mill at Cressbrook (1815): with its central pediment and cupola, and the Apprentice House with Gothick front nearby, it might almost pass for a large stable block at a country house. The railway viaducts at Chinley are monumental; the railway stations at Cromford, at Matlock Bath and at Wingfield are all of special charm. All these help to give Derbyshire its highly individual character—and no mention has yet been made of its great houses.

GREAT HOUSES and GREAT FAMILIES

Derbyshire is essentially the county of great houses. It can claim more than any other county of the old and astonishing family homes whose names are bound up with the history of England. Without pausing to think, a whole list rolls off the tongue—Melbourne, Sudbury, Calke Abbey, Catton, Locko, Radburne, Tissington, Hopton, Renishaw, Elvaston, Foremark, Ogston, Barlborough. And apart from all these, and many other smaller manor houses, there are Chatsworth, Haddon, Hardwick, Bolsover, and Kedleston supreme above the rest. The houses themselves are astonishing enough; but without their history, and the history of the families who have tended them for centuries, they lose half their significance and appeal. It would be a mistake to pass through Derbyshire without giving oneself time to imbibe a little of the history of the dynasties which still stand for so much in the life of the county.

Three of these great houses owe most of their

importance to a single woman, the redoubtable Bess of Hardwick. This woman was the daughter of one John Hardwick of Hardwick Hall near Ault Hucknall, and was born in 1518. Her home was even then an enormous place, but the family appears to have been badly off, and Bess was from the very first imbued with a passionate and abiding determination to better her worldly position by fair means or foul. Her first move in this direction was a false one, for she married as a child one Barlow, a neighbour and social equal; but it was rapidly retrieved, for Barlow died almost immediately after, leaving her a widow at fifteen, with a large addition to her wealth, and to her wordly wisdom. It was sixteen years before she married again, and this time she made no mistake, for she fastened upon a Cavendish, a member of one of the families who were swallowing up the monastic estates as fast as they were being confiscated. It was true that he had been married twice before, but that hardly mattered, as there were no male heirs. As Treasurer of the Chamber, Sir William Cavendish was in on the ground floor of the enormous racket of monastic dispossession, and his properties augmented every month. At the time of his marriage these lands were mostly situated in the southern counties, but Bess soon changed all that. Her husband, she resolved, was from now on going to reside in her county; so the abbeys and priories and convents were duly sold and the money reinvested in the wide lands of Derbyshire. Among their new estates, Bess decided on Chatsworth for a residence, and bought it in 1549 for £600. There was already a fine house on the property, but not fine enough for Lady Cavendish. Almost at once she began to build a new one, and in the course of fourteen years she spent £80,000 on an immense house in the finest domestic style of the period, of which not a trace now remains. But alas, it was scarcely begun when Sir William Cavendish departed this life, leaving Bess a widow again at the age of thirty-nine, with three sons and three daughters and an enormous estate in her own absolute possession.

This time she could afford to marry whom she pleased, and she decided upon one Sir William St Loe, a rising soldier and the possessor of "divers fair lordships in Gloucestershire, which in articles of marriage she took care should be settled on her and her heirs". It was a sound arrangement: the husband was detained in London by his duties, while the wife continued furiously building and buying in Derbyshire. But Chatsworth was still unfinished when St Loe also died, leaving Bess a widow for the third time, the right side of fifty, and in enjoyment of his whole estate, to the exclusion of his former daughters and his brothers.

Her fourth attempt was the finest of them all, for in 1568 she married George Talbot, sixth Earl of Shrewsbury, Lord High Steward, Lord Lieutenant of Yorkshire, Nottinghamshire, and Derbyshire, Knight of the Garter, and Lord of Worksop, Welbeck, Bolsover, Sheffield, Tutbury, Wingfield, and Rufford. Moreover, to make doubly sure of this superb inheritance, she insisted on marrying one son and one daughter of her Cavendish offspring to an infant daughter and son respectively of her new husband's by a previous marriage. By this masterly manoeuvre, she secured to herself by triple bonds a position as magnificent as any woman in England could claim. And within a year her great private position as a chatelaine became a position of public trust, for Lord Shrewsbury was entrusted with the stringent and exacting custody of the fugitive Mary Queen of Scots. Poor Shrewsbury not only had to spy upon the Queen of Scots, but was, himself, constantly spied upon by the Queen of England. And little thanks he got from anyone. Bess, indeed, had altogether the best of the arrangement. While Shrewsbury could never be a day away from the Queen of Scots, Bess was rampaging over the Midlands, building half a dozen houses at a time, spending Shrewsbury's income many times over.

25

Hardwick Hall

It was not till 1584—two years before Fotheringay—that Shrewsbury was finally rid of Mary. By this time he was heartily tired of playing second fiddle to his wife. The few years that remained to him were mostly spent in law-suits, trying to protect his reputation against her slanders, and trying to recover some of the vast possessions of which she had stripped him. In 1591 he died, a broken and worn-out man.

Bess was now seventy-three, and at the height of her worldly fortunes. The entire belongings of the Cavendishes and the Talbots, as well as the Barlows and the St Loes, were in her own absolute

disposition. And to them was now added an inheritance of her own—Hardwick, her birthplace, which descended to her in her old age. But, old as she was, she was not yet going to relax her grip on her belongings. She was still building furiously: she began to rebuild both Worksop and Bolsover, she started a large new house called Oldcotes; but her principal activity was the rebuilding of Hardwick Hall. This was her greatest occupation between her seventieth and eightieth years. She died in 1608: with her usual foresight she had erected her own monument and epitaph in Derby church, well knowing that nobody would give twopence to this object when she was dead.

◁ The terrace at Bolsover

29

The new Earl of Shrewsbury, her stepson and son-in-law, inherited Sheffield, Rufford and Worksop. None of these is in Derbyshire. Her eldest son, Henry Cavendish she loathed, because he had taken Lord Shrewsbury's part against her: his portion was Tutbury, an old castle on a high hill overlooking the southern valley of the Dove, in Staffordshire. He died without lawful issue. Bess Hardwick's second son, William Cavendish, was the apple of her eye. To him descended both Chatsworth and Hardwick, and he later became the first Earl of Devonshire.

Of the sixteenth-century Chatsworth nothing now remains except Queen Mary's Bower, a moated enclosure near the bridge, where the Queen of Scots is reputed to have spent a great deal of her heavy time. Hardwick, on the other hand, is almost exactly as Bess left it. Almost everything in the house is contemporary, and everything from the proud initials E.S., which are worked into the parapet, is saturated with her personality. Its huge windows gleam in the sun: "Hardwick Hall, more glass than wall." "E.S.", Elizabeth Shrewsbury, proclaim the coroneted parapets; it is a supremely self-confident house.

To Charles Cavendish, her youngest son, Bess allocated Welbeck and Bolsover. He inherited her passion for building to the full. Welbeck he rebuilt entirely the year after her death, while at Bolsover he continued the rebuilding that she had begun. His family became Dukes of Newcastle, before uniting with the Dutch dynasty of the Bentincks, who survive as Dukes of Portland. Bolsover deserves a visit; much of it is in ruins: immense fireplaces stand open to the elements. It can hardly be expected that the spirit of Bess Hardwick should not roam the courtyard at night, raging that such a palace should be left roofless while a jewel remains to pawn.

The descendants of William Cavendish prospered exceedingly as Earls of Devonshire. They were faithful to the Royalist cause in the Civil Wars, but the fourth Earl was no friend to Charles II, or still less to James II. With other disaffected peers he used to meet secretly at the Cock at Whittington, where the overthrow of James II was planned. As early as May 1687 he put his name to an invitation to William of Orange. When William actually landed, the Earl secured Derby with 500 men and marched on Nottingham before going to meet the invader and seek his reward. These rewards were unsparingly granted. Offices and honours showered upon him, culminating in a dukedom. To signalise his sense of the permanence of the revolution, the new duke set about building a new Chatsworth. He decided to build a palace rather than a house.

Of the house itself an account is given in the Gazetteer. It was the sixth duke who employed Wyatville to make the great additions in the early nineteenth century. Not content with these additions, he embarked on the most magnificent series of works in the garden. In 1826 he had been impressed by the abilities of a lad whom he had found working in the grounds of his villa at Chiswick, Joseph Paxton. Paxton was made head gardener at Chatsworth, and given a free hand. His ideas were as lavish as those of the duke, with whom he established a relation of perfect equality; the two of them travelled everywhere together. One of Paxton's achievements was the Emperor Fountain, made to amuse the Czar of Russia, which is 267 feet high; another was the model village of Edensor in the park. But Paxton's masterpiece was the famous conservatory, "the glory of Chatsworth" as Murray's Handbook calls it. It was 276 feet long, 123 feet wide, 60 feet high, and covered an acre of ground. It contained forty miles of sash bars, and was heated by seven miles of hot pipes, fed with fuel by a subterranean tramway half a mile long. One could drive through it in a carriage, admiring "a forest of tropical foliage, palms and cedars, pines and ferns". Alas, the glory of Chatsworth is laid low! During the Great War it was decided that the upkeep of seven miles of hot pipes set a bad example to the nation. The conservatory was demolished, and present-day visitors have to put up with the house.

Paxton, as every schoolboy knows, went on from strength to strength. His design for the 1851

Exhibition, based on an enlarged edition of his conservatory and drawn up in nine days, was accepted, and became known to the world as the Crystal Palace. Paxton was knighted, and sat for many years in Parliament. The Crystal Palace was one of the foundation stones of modern architecture.

The second great family of Derbyshire is the family of Manners of Haddon Hall, whose head is the Duke of Rutland. Haddon Hall stands fairly close to the road from Rowsley to Bakewell. You come upon it suddenly, motoring along the banks of the Wye; there before you is a building so entirely a part of the woods and meadows that you might easily not have noticed it at all. It is the most enigmatic of buildings. It is difficult to say whether it is large or small, close to you or far away. Its detail is small, yet its extent is vast; its proportions are light and elegant, yet its construction is massive. You come closer, and the mystery grows. It is a fortress made of gossamer, a castle as welcoming as a cottage. It has no date: it is both very old and very young. But where exactly its magic lies you must determine for yourself.

At the Conquest Haddon was granted by William to his bastard, William Peveril, together with the immense territory which centred round the Peak Castle at Castleton. But the Peverils, though their name lingered, were short-lived. In 1155 the honour of Peveril was forfeited, and shortly after William de Vernon acquired the manor of Haddon: henceforth the history of the place is bound up with the names of Vernon and Manners. The Vernons of Haddon were a great family: they are found as Speakers of the House of Commons, as Treasurers of Calais, even as Constables of England. The grandest of them all was the last, Sir George Vernon, who flourished in the reign of Henry VIII, and was known as King of the Peak, on account of his magnificent manner of living and his superb hospitality. He was lord of thirty manors, and eighty retainers waited in his hall.

Sir George had a younger brother, Sir John, who lived at Sudbury, on the Derby–Uttoxeter road, where his descendant, Lord Vernon, still

lives. For himself he had no male heir, but only two daughters. The elder was engaged to a son of Lord Derby's; the younger, Dorothy, was in love with John Manners, the second son of the Earl of Rutland, of Belvoir Castle. According to tradition, the King of the Peak frowned on this latter alliance; John Manners had to disguise himself as a forester to have access to his beloved, Dorothy Vernon was kept under lock and key; and one night while a great ball was being held in celebration of her sister's wedding, she slipped out of a side door, along the terrace, down the long flight of stairs, and over the bridge to where Manners was waiting to carry her off to a village in Leicestershire where they were married. The story has always flourished in the popular imagination, and visitors used to be duly shown the ballroom, the door, the terrace, and the steps which had been hallowed by such a romantic episode. But, in point of fact, all of them—ballroom, door, terrace and steps—were built in later years by the very John Manners who is supposed to have been waiting at the bottom of the hill; the marriage was as sensible from the worldly point of view as most sixteenth-century marriages, and Sir George Vernon, if he had disapproved would hardly have bequeathed his property to the miscreant daughter to the exclusion both of her elder sister and his own younger brother.

In 1567 Sir George Vernon died, and Haddon became, what it has ever since remained, a part of the Manners estates. Dorothy Manners only survived her father seventeen years, but Sir John lived to a ripe age. They are buried side by side in Bakewell church. Their respective crests, the boar's head and the peacock, are to be found all over the building. Their heirs inherited Haddon Hall from one side, and from the other side Belvoir near Grantham, and the earldom of Rutland. The family sided with the Parliament in the Civil Wars, so that Haddon escaped the savage iconoclasm of Sir John Gell, who destroyed so many fine houses in Derbyshire, and would probably have been overjoyed to destroy this one, the loveliest of all. At the Restoration the Rutlands

Kedleston; the south front ▷

32

were not disturbed in their possessions. But their tastes had altered. They came to prefer the solid comforts of Belvoir. Haddon was one of those houses where the guests have to traverse moonlit courtyards on the way to dinner, or to bed, or on lesser errands. It was not good enough for a courtier of William III; still less was it good enough for a duke, as the seventh earl became in 1703, Just over the hill the old Chatsworth was being pulled down by the Devonshires. In its place, wing after endless wing, arose that stupendous pile, the Palace of the Peak. This was more than the Rutlands could stand. They abandoned the unequal rivalry. They dismantled the old house inside and moved to Belvoir, lock, stock and barrel, taking with them a household of one hundred souls.

From that time onwards Haddon Hall was just a show-place. Horace Walpole dismisses it as "an abandoned old castle of the Rutlands". To the eighteenth century, so comfortable and so sensible, it was nothing more. But with the romantic revival it crept back into popular admiration: while so much spoof romanticism was being written and painted, here was the real thing, with every lattice and crenellation and every self-sown oak tree in its own romantic place. It became a place of pilgrimage. With the coming of the steam railroad to Rowsley, thousands and tens of thousands came every year to wonder and rhapsodise over chapel and tower and minstrels' gallery. The Dorothy Vernon legend was invented; ghosts were freely imagined; rooms were given the sort of names that tourists love.

It was left to the present century to decide that Haddon should be brought to life once more. In 1912 the ninth Duke of Rutland began this great undertaking. It was an immense task: 200 years had done their worst, and it proved a full lifetime's work.

The last house to be dealt with here will be the great house of Kedleston and its owners the Curzons. Kedleston stands some four miles north west of Derby, in a large park watered by

the Markeaton Brook. It is as fine an eighteenth-century house as any in England, the masterpiece of Robert Adam. It had only been up twelve years when Johnson and Boswell drove over from Ashbourne to see it. Boswell was overwhelmed by the extensive park, the huge oaks, the deer, the lake—"in short the grand group of objects agitated and distended my mind in a most agreeable manner. 'One should think (said I) that the proprietor of all this *must* be happy.'—'Nay, Sir, (said Johnson) all this excludes but one evil—poverty.'"

Kedleston is a house of superb beauty and, like Hardwick, an architectural unity, filled with the splendid furniture and pictures originally intended for it. The church, too, which nestles incongruously beside it, is of special interest for the curious evidence it presents of a typical English landowning family. The Curzons of Kedleston go back 850 years, and include even a Cardinal Curzon, who died on the Crusades. Part of the church itself is Norman, and the tombs of the various Curzons date almost from the Conquest. From simple brasses to Jacobean effigies the evolution is continuous; from the elaborate sculpture of Rysbrack you are carried on in unbroken sequence to the monument of a Victorian Curzon who combined the duties of lord of the manor and incumbent of the parish. And then suddenly this old but unambitious family produces a great man. Simplicity blossoms forth into splendour: a great north aisle, designed by Bodley, with stained glass by F. C. Eden, enshrines George Nathaniel, Marquis Curzon of Kedleston, Cabinet Minister, Foreign Secretary, Viceroy of India:

"In divers offices and in many lands
As Explorer, Writer, Administrator
   and ruler of men
He sought to serve his country
And add honour to an ancient name."

DERBYSHIRE TODAY

Derbyshire is fortunate in that so many of its great houses still survive. Indeed it is possible that the ruin of yet another—Sutton Scarsdale—nobly saved after the last war by Sir Osbert Sitwell, may be taken over by the Ministry of Public Building and Works, and preserved as an ancient monument. The county has been less fortunate in the survival of some of its industrial monuments. In many a valley, or back street of some murky town, there stand empty mills or factories—monumental buildings often, crumbling and till recently little appreciated. Interest in industrial archaeology is something comparatively new: for the enthusiast there are endless possibilities —in Cromford, for instance, in New Mills, Glossop, Belper, Swadlincote, in any of the towns or villages of the Erewash Valley, and in many out of the way dales or valleys. Frank Nixon's admirable *Industrial Archaeology of Derbyshire* (David & Charles, 1969) is a perfect guide. Unfortunately Jedediah Strutt's splendid old mills (1780) at Milford have already been demolished. Another sad loss of the last few years has been the run-down of the Midland Railway.

The Midland was Derbyshire's special railway. After endless squabbling in the early years the North Midland, the Midland Counties, and the Birmingham & Derby Junction Railways were united to form the Midland Railway in 1844, and Derby was its headquarters. The great Midland system in time reached Manchester in the north-west, Carlisle and Edinburgh in the north, London in the south, and Bristol in the south-west. Derby was its physical centre—London, as it were, was only at the end of a branch. The administrative offices were at Derby, so were the locomotive works, the carriage works, the wagon works, the signal works.

Of the great railway lines of England, one of the most striking was the line from Derby to Manchester. Its construction was achieved against great obstacles. The first obstacle was the fierce opposition of the M.R.'s great rival, the L. & N.W.R. Still greater obstacles were met in building the line itself. Great viaducts had to be constructed, great tunnels bored (Dove Holes Tunnel alone cost some £136,000), long cuttings made, the line itself poised at times for miles on end on narrow ledges of rock, numberless bridges built (near Belper there are no less than ten in a mile), steep gradients undertaken. It was a marvel of engineering. At Bakewell the line achieved a great panoramic sweep of the wide valley of the Wye: soon after, the train shot out of Headstone Tunnel to run high over Monsal Dale. Professor Jack Simmons has likened this most beautiful part of the journey to a "series of rapidly-shifting cinema shots through one of the most remarkable stretches of mountain country in England". Now this wonderful line is closed—the great labour of an age thrown away—and a small diesel car will take passengers to Matlock, and no further.

Elsewhere, too, lines are being ripped up, and many a sombre valley looks grimmer still for the loss of its railway. Great wastelands appear in the old industrial regions of the Erewash.

In Derbyshire as elsewhere in 1971 desolation assumes other shapes too. Nasty houses are built of materials foreign to the district. Old houses are jazzed up by owners with more money than taste, innocent little cottages made pretentious with bogus carriage-lamps, bogus cart-wheels turned into bogus garden gates. The streets in the towns are becoming anonymous as the same supermarkets rear the same shop fronts as in every other town in England, and the brewery companies cast the spell of a dead sameness over their tied public houses. This is desolation indeed. But the great moorland survives, the vast open stretches of solitary peakland are unassailable, and the magic of Dovedale can never be destroyed by the motor car.

Two requests, however, might in conclusion be made on behalf of the traveller in Derbyshire in 1971. The first is an appeal to the County Council: Derbyshire is a county of broken signposts. Pleasant as it is to be lost in Derbyshire, it can be disappointing to be unable to find the road to some obscure village. The second is an appeal to the clergy: Derbyshire is a county of locked churches. This may indeed be a sad necessity in the England of today, but where a church has perforce to be locked, a notice in the porch to explain where to obtain the key would save disappointment and frustration. It would help the Church, too, in its great task of preserving this part of England's heritage.

Gazetteer

The number after each entry refers to the square on the map following page 124 where the place is situated.

Alderwasley (11). Pronounced "Allersley". In high country, overlooking the Derwent Valley. The Hall is a grand but plain three-storeyed Georgian house, commanding a view across the valley up to Crich Stand. It is now an R.C. prep school, but was the home of the Hurts, an old established county family, who became pioneer iron-masters and industrialists in the eighteenth century. It was Francis Hurt who built the pair of iron furnaces at Morley Park near Heage. There is a small sixteenth-century chapel, long disused; and close to the Hall gates is the imposing new church of 1850. Interior a little bleak: tidy Victorian furnishings.

Alfreton (9). A somewhat drab industrial town, close to the Notts border, and surrounded by coal-fields and iron works. Great new by-pass road, opened 1970. There are few buildings to note, except for the eighteenth-century George Hotel. The street to the W leads to the church. Perp. W tower and large clerestoried nave. Mural monument in chancel to John Ormond and his wife Joan Chaworth (1507): the Latin inscription contains long genealogical details. In N aisle monument to Anthony Morewood (d. 1636) who bought the manor of Alfreton, and at the E end of this aisle a very fine monument, with superb details, to George Morewood (d. 1742).

To the W of the church stands Alfreton Hall: this has recently been bought by the town from the More-wood family for use as a public park. Part of the house has been demol-ished: large nineteenth-century add-itions had been made to an eighteenth-century core, probably the work of Francis Smith of Warwick.

Alkmonton (11). Tiny village in the gentle country south of Ashbourne. Little flint church of 1843, with spiky bell turret. Norman font from previous church.

Alport (11). At the entrance to Lathkill Dale: here the Lathkill joins the River Bradford. Eighteenth-century bridge. Old lead-mining area until nineteenth century: the mines and other early industrial ventures explain the presence of several good seventeenth- and eighteenth-century houses. Walking country—to Hart-hill Moor, and the Dale itself. Nine Stones Circle on Harthill Moor.

Alsop-en-le-Dale (11). A narrow lane plunges off the Ashbourne–Buxton road, and comes to Alsop. Diminu-tive, well-treed village. Small Norman church, somewhat Victorianised, with Victorian Norman tower, and extraordinary nineteenth-century square Gothick pulpit within. Opposite the church, early seven-teenth-century Alsop Hall, very tall and narrow, has mullioned windows. Exhilarating country.

Ambergate (11). Here the Amber joins the Derwent. Small Gothic church (1891). Marooned among railway lines Francis Thompson's station survives, unused.

Ashbourne (11). One of the best towns in Derbyshire. It is often called the Gateway to the Peak: here the gentle undulating country of the south gives way to the severe limestone plateau of the north, and hedges give way to stone walls. Dovedale, and the peakland country that stretches up to Buxton and beyond, are easily accessible.

Church Street and St John Street form the main artery: both are lined with old houses. St John Street (to the E) leads up to the Market Square: Church Street (to the W) to the Parish Church.

In St John Street pride of place goes to the Green Man Hotel, with its inn-sign across the street, and its arched open entrance leading into its courtyard behind. Johnson and Boswell stayed here on several occasions: Boswell thought it a "very good inn", and its mistress a "mighty civil gentlewoman". It is still delightful, as it has escaped the pretentious modernisation so often now meted out to these good old hotels.

In the Market Place James III was proclaimed King when Prince Charles Edward reached Ashbourne in 1745. In the Green Man is an old picture of the Square as the scene of the "kick-off" of the famous Shrove Tuesday football game—a kind of free-for-all, with the two goals, two mills, some three miles apart. Up the hill from the market place is St John's (1871) a former proprietary chapel, originally established by the Wrights of Osmaston.

In Church Street are good houses: particular mention must be made of Nos. 16–22, the Clergy Widows' Almshouse, founded in 1753, a fine Georgian composition round a small open courtyard; Nos. 24–26 with giant Ionic pilasters (alas, half the façade now spoilt by shop fronts); No. 49, a plain three-storeyed Georgian house, with a flight of steps up to a pedimented doorcase; the Grey House, the finest house in the street, with bay windows, Tuscan porch and central Venetian window; and the Mansion opposite, with many features in common with the Grey House, but built of brick—the home of Johnson's friend, Dr Taylor. At the far end is the splendid front of the Grammar School, built between 1583 and 1589, with its symmetrical front of six gables. And now we are at the church.

This is one of the finest in the county, and the spire (212 ft) dominates the scene. The earliest part of the church is the long E chancel with lancet windows: there are more lancets in the N transept. The nave arcade and the great windows in the transepts and else-where are Dec. Notable carving on nave pillars. Both transepts have grand E aisles, built as family chapels. The tower and spire are early fourteenth-century. Inside, the arrangement of the nave is strange: there is no N aisle, and the heavily

37

buttressed base of the tower impinges into the nave on the N side, and the arcade impinges on the crossing arch on the S. There is a little thirteenth-century grisaille glass in the N transept, but the Victorian glass predominates. Windows of 1861 in chancel, abused by Ruskin as "the worst piece of base Birmingham manufacture" that he had seen. Windows elsewhere by Burlison and Grylls (1872) and Hardman (1874), and E window by Kempe.

There is a great array of tombs to Cockaynes and Bradbournes of the fifteenth and sixteenth centuries. These include Sir Thomas Cockayne, one of the founders of the Grammar School (d. 1592). The Cockaynes faded in the seventeenth century, and were followed by the Boothby baronets. That to Penelope (*aet.* 5) by Thomas Banks (1791) is well known, as is the inscription—"the unfortunate parents ventured their all on this frail bark, and the wreck was total". The Boothbys subsequently left Ashbourne, and even their great house is now gone.

Ashford-in-the-Water (8). One of the prettiest villages in Derbyshire. Three bridges cross the River Wye, of which the best is Sheepwash Bridge, with stone enclosure for washing sheep. A second is dated 1664. The church was largely rebuilt in 1870, but the tower is mediaeval, and over the S door is a Norman tympanum. Jacobean pulpit. Big Royal Arms of 1724, painted. Three maidens' funeral garlands (eighteenth century) in S aisle. Tablet to Henry Watson, son of Samuel Watson of Heanor (q.v.), who established marble works here in 1748. His son was White Watson (see Hassop and Bakewell). Ashford Hall is a dignified stone Georgian house.

Ashover (8). High up on the moors, between Chesterfield and Matlock. A light railway (constructed about fifty years ago) used to carry spar from the Ashover quarry to Clay Cross, and—in early days—passengers. Some of the track is still visible in the valley below the village, and a number of old trucks lie sadly in

their derelict sidings. The Crispin Inn, the old school, and the church make an attractive village centre. The Inn, according to the long printed inscription over its door, "probably dates from the year 1416, when Thomas Babington of Dethick and several men of Asher returned from the Battle of Agincourt which was fought on St Crispin's Day". The School is 1845 Tudor, with projecting porch, a charming building, alas! derelict. Old lime trees (marked IW 1778) and fine table tombs line the way to the church, which is largely Perp., battlemented, with handsome tower and spire traditionally built by Thomas Babington in the early fifteenth century. Notable twelfth-century lead font, one of the finest in England. Screen, bearing the arms of Babington and Fitzherbert, erected by Thomas Babington in 1511. Seventeenth-century pulpit. Great alabaster altar

Norman tympanum, AULT HUCKNALL

tomb of Thomas Babington (d. 1518) and his wife Edith Fitzherbert, sister of Sir Anthony Fitzherbert, the judge (see Norbury). The many coats of arms are coloured. Sixteenth-century brasses in chancel. Two eighteenth-century tablets with amusing inscriptions: one to Francis Parkes (1713) records that "by his natural genius and great industry he became wonderful proficient in the gentler art of painting"; another to David Wall, "whose superior performance on the bassoon endeared him to an extensive musical acquaintance, and whose social life closed in 1796".

A mile to the E stand the ivy-clad ruins of Eastwood Hall, blown up by the Roundheads in 1646. It was until 1623 the home of the Reresby family. A mile to the S is Overton Hall, in a remote position down a long drive in a rocky park, a tall square early eighteenth-century house, surrounded

◁ Decorated tracery, ASHBOURNE

by out-buildings. It was one of the homes of Sir Joseph Banks, the explorer and naturalist: he inherited it from his mother. It is now an old people's home.

Aston-on-Trent (15). The Georgian Hall (1735) is now a hospital, and has been much enlarged.

Church with Norman tower (pinnacled upper stage Perp.). The chief attraction is the lofty chancel, with tall straight-headed Dec. windows. Dignified, clerestoried nave; Victorian canopied pulpit; thirteenth-century font; fifteenth-century alabaster tomb with effigies (unknown); nineteenth-century tablets to Holdens and Clowes; and in a glass case an eighteenth-century bassoon.

Much new housing in village.

Atlow (11). Little hamlet, lost in the back roads near Hulland. Gay little Victorian church of 1874—stone outside, brick and stone inside, enlivened with many bright coloured tiles.

Ault Hucknall (9). At the gates of Hardwick. In a back lane, overlooking the park, stands the church. There is an early Norman tympanum built into the W front, but the regular Perp. battlemented exterior does not prepare the visitor for the interior, primitive and full of mystery. The N arcade is Norman: the tiny arches in the crossing of the central tower are Norman, or perhaps earlier. Through this narrow opening the high altar and its sanctuary lamp are just visible. There is sixteenth-century stained glass in the SE chapel, and below the E window is the very unusual tomb (1627) to the first Countess of Devonshire. On the floor of this chapel is the inscription to Thomas Hobbes the philosopher: "Condita hic sunt ossa Thomas Hobbes, Malmsburiensis, qui per multos annos servivit duobus Devoniae comitibus, patri et filio. Vir probus et fama eruditionis, domi forisque bene cognitus. Obiit Anno Dom. 1679 mensis Decembris die 4°, aetatis suae 91." "Here are deposited the bones of Thomas Hobbes, of Malmesbury, who for many years served two Earls of

Devonshire, father and son. A man of integrity and distinguished for his learning, famous at home and abroad. He died Dec. 4 1679 A.D. *aet.* 91." In the N aisle is the tablet to Robert Hackett, Keeper of Hardwick Park, who died December 1st 1703:

"Long had he chas'd
The red and fallow deer,
But death's cold dart
At last has fix'd him here."

Bakewell (8). The town is beautifully set, with the River Wye running through the valley, high hills to N, E and W—the valley broadening out towards Haddon Hall, and the church dominating everything from its high ground. There are few houses of special note, but the appearance of the whole town is very agreeable.

The bridge over the river is fourteenth century: Bridge Street leads up to the good-looking late-Georgian Rutland Arms Hotel, which is the centre of the town. The old Market Hall is late seventeenth century; the old Town Hall was built in 1709. The new Town Hall was built in 1890 (G. E. Statham of Manchester, architect). In Bath Street is the Bath House, built for the 1st Duke of Rutland in 1697: the chalybeate spring bubbles up under a low vault. In the early nineteenth century this house was the home of White Watson, who was superintendent of the bath, as well as sculptor (see Ashford-in-the-Water).

The approach to the church is impressive: the long arms of chancel and transept, crowned by the unusual octagonal central tower and spire, are a splendid sight. Remains of Saxon cross in churchyard, and many more Saxon fragments in S porch and elsewhere. Norman W front—W window fifteenth-century insertion. The nave was largely rebuilt in 1852; the fourteenth-century tower and spire also underwent a careful rebuilding at this time: the result is a somewhat sombre Victorianised interior. There are, however, interesting monuments in S transept—particularly Sir George Vernon (d. 1567) and Sir John Manners (d. 1584) and his wife Dorothy Vernon. Also a monument to Sir Godfrey Foljambe (d. 1377) and his wife, who look out under a

wonderfully decorated ogee arch, as out of a little balcony. Early fourteenth-century octagonal font.

A little to the N out of the town stands the early seventeenth-century Holme Hall, built by the Eyre family, with mullioned windows and central porch projection. To the S, along the road to Haddon, is Burton Closes, a house of 1845 by Pugin— but, alas, desecrated by "development".

Ballidon (11). Small hamlet close to Bradbourne, chiefly famous for its quarries: you will meet great lorries bearing the name BALLIDON across the country. There is a tiny church in a field to the S, a much-restored Norman structure.

Bamford (5). Peak countryside; a paradise for walkers to Bamford Edge and the Ladybower reservoir. Beautiful church of 1861 by Butterfield: tall needle-like spire, and other Butterfieldian features.

Barlborough (6). Industrial NE Derbyshire: there is a new roundabout at the intersection of the A616 and the A619, and traffic roars by on the M1, a quarter of a mile away below. The church was much restored in 1899, but there is some mediaeval work, including a late Norman N arcade. Georgian rectory opposite.

N of the village stands Barlborough Hall ("the House Next Door" in Sir Osbert Sitwell's autobiography). Tall and grey, turreted, romantic and beautiful at the end of its long lime avenue, it is one of the smaller "progeny houses", and belongs to a group that includes Hardwick, Heath Old Hall in Yorkshire, and Wotton Lodge in Staffordshire. It is dated 1583 and was built for Lord Justice Francis Rodes. Its design is attributed to Robert Smythson. It has been much altered inside, and is now the prep. school for Mount St Mary's College.

Further N there stands by itself Park Hall, a mid-seventeenth-century, three-storeyed, gabled house, now a country club.

Barlow (5). High on the moors to the NW of Chesterfield, with views. The best time to visit Barlow is in the middle of August, when the celebrated well-dressing takes place, on the Wednesday in the octave of St Laurence, the patron saint. The whole village is then en fête: the well is gorgeously decorated with flowers, and flags fly.

Little Norman church, beautifully furnished. Aisleless nave, with little eighteenth-century bellcote. Plain Norman chancel arch. Norman-revival chancel of 1867. The Lady's Quire, or Lady Chapel, was added to the S of the nave in 1340, as a chantry for the Barlow family. The Barlow (or Barley) family took their name from the place, and there is an alabaster tomb slab to Robert Barley and his wife, 1467. The chapel was restored by Sir Montague Barlow in 1936. The best-known member of the family was perhaps the young squire, Robert Barlow, who became first husband to Bess of Hardwick when he was fourteen, and she fifteen, in 1532.

To the W of the village stands the gabled Woodseats Hall (sixteenth–seventeenth century), which was the home of the Mower family. Arthur Mower was agent to the Barley family, and kept a remarkable diary from 1555 to 1610: the fifty-two volumes are now in the British Museum. In 1608 he records the death of Bess of Hardwick: "she was a great purchaser and getter together of much goods. She builded Chattesworth, Hardwick and Owlcotes, and was a greate builder and purchaser."

Barrow-on-Trent (14). Fanciful little Gothick lodge at the centre of the village, surviving from the burnt-down hall. Many modern bungalows on the site of the house. Pretty lane to the river, and to the church. This, with its square tower, is light and airy with plain glass windows—a large Dec. window under the tower, and a Georgian E window. Distinguished N arcade (thirteenth-century piers). Clerestory windows in wooden frames. Black-and-white farmhouse at W end of church.

Barton Blount (14). In a small park to the N of Church Broughton is Barton Blount, an eighteenth-century house, with a chapel alongside. This ancient manor belonged in the Middle Ages to the Blounts, Lords Mountjoy: in the sixteenth century it passed

by purchase to the Merrys, a recusant family, who held it till the eighteenth; it has since changed hands a number of times. Behind the mid-eighteenth-century stone S front is the original gatehouse, encased in stone in the nineteenth century. The little mediaeval chapel has passed through many vicissitudes: the early eighteenth-century S porch is handsome.

Baslow (8). A justly famous beauty spot, close to the N gates of Chatsworth, with two bridges over the Derwent. The Peacock, the Devonshire Arms and other hostelries serve walkers and tourists. The church with its broach spire is set close to the old bridge and the river. The E face of the clock has round its face VICTORIA 1897: the N side has an eighteenth-century face. Interior decently and comfortably Victorian.

Beeley (8). Small stone village close to the S entrance to Chatsworth; a singularly unexpected pair of traffic lights guards the entrance to the park. Much "estate" building of the mid nineteenth century. Church, with Norman S door, was much restored in 1882. Beeley Hall is a tall early seventeenth-century house, now a farm. The road to the E leads up to the desolate moors above Chatsworth.

Beighton (6). Close to Sheffield and suburbanised, but preserving something of the ancient village. Perp. church with pinnacled tower, in good position with views towards the city, and beautifully furnished for Anglo-Catholic worship. Florentine marble reredos. Handsome early Georgian stone manor house opposite, with old farm buildings alongside.

Belper (11). The name is a corruption of Beau Repaire—a charming name for a hunting lodge—and Edmund Crouchback, Earl of Lancaster, second son of Henry III, had a hunting lodge here. It was he who supposedly founded the old chapel of St John Baptist (in The Butts) c. 1250: this has been much altered and rebuilt in the seventeenth, and again in the nineteenth, centuries.

The town as it is now owes everything to the Strutt family, whose founder, Jedediah, started here in 1776 one of the first cotton mills in

England. He took his power from the River Derwent, and his coal from the great coalfields in the vicinity. The oldest surviving mill is that near the bridge, and it dates from 1797. Enormous new buildings were added, in the brightest of red brick, in the nineteenth century, and these dominate the town. Near here is Christ Church (1849), an attractive great barn-like church: Victorian grisaille glass, W gallery with Lady Chapel beneath—the clear glass windows give good views to open country—High Altar with reredos and tester. Splendid brass handles to the main door! The vicarage stands next door: notice how the oriel window on the first floor serves as a focal point for the streets that meet here.

These surrounding streets contain interesting early industrial architecture (e.g. George Brettle's warehouse, 1834), and the villas and terraces of the workers climb the hills. In this upper town is St Peter's (1824) by Habershon, built as the new parish church of the town. It is in the Commissioners' style, with W tower and galleried interior. Monument to Geroge Brettle (1835) by Westmacott.

Biggin (7). Lonely village in Peak country, close to Hartington. Stone walls. Windswept trees. Early Victorian Gothic church by Shellard (1845). At Newhaven, on the A515 is the Newhaven House Hotel, a big, late Georgian building, erected by the 5th Duke of Devonshire.

Birchover (8). Romantic craggy country near Stanton-in-the-Peak. In a deep wooded valley stands a little church called the Jesus Chapel, founded in the early eighteenth century by the Revd Thomas Eyre, of Rowtor Hall (now the rectory), with a small endowment. Subsequently both chapel and house became ruinous—the chapel being used as a cheese-store—till rebuilt by Mr Thornhill of Stanton in 1869. Strange carvings and decorations inside, and barge-style paintings by a previous incumbent. Norman fragments near door.

The Rowtor Rocks tower above, and there are great outcrops of granite rock on Harthill Moor to the W. The area became associated with a form of Druidical religion in the eighteenth century. But in the face of Cratcliffe Rocks is a hermit's cave, with a crucifix carved out of the granite.

Blackwell (9). In colliery country. Not far from the church is the farmhouse where Jedediah Strutt lived and perfected his stocking frame. The church has one circular pier of the twelfth century preserved, but is chiefly of the nineteenth century. Large fragment of Saxon cross in churchyard.

Bolsover (9). Bolsover Castle is the third of the three great Cavendish houses in Derbyshire. It shares with Hardwick a certain strangeness, and its ascription to a member of the great Smythson family of architects. John and Huntingdon Smythson, son and grandson respectively of the great Robert, are both buried in the churchyard—they died in 1634 and 1648.

The town of Bolsover is of little consequence, but the position of the Castle looking over the great, open, blackened vale of Scarsdale is memorable indeed. From the terrace it is possible to see the towers of Hardwick to the SW, the gaunt ruin of Sutton Scarsdale to the W—and everywhere the collieries, with their smoke, railway sidings, miners' cottages and, now, the M1. From below, and even from a distance, the view of the long line of the Castle buildings, terminating with the keep, stretching along the steep brow of the hill, is memorable too. On a summer evening the buildings, brilliant white in colour, shine like a fairy castle.

And a fairy castle it is: there had been a castle here in Norman times, but what we see now is a rebuilding (1613–16) by Sir Charles Cavendish (youngest son of Bess) in a consciously romantic taste. Mr Mark Girouard has described this seventeenth-century romantic movement in his book on Robert Smythson, and links Bolsover with Wollaton and Lulworth, as well as with Hardwick, Barlborough and Chastleton.

Inside the keep is a series of remarkable rooms: the vaulted Hall, the Pillar Room, the Star Chamber—all with ornate chimney-pieces, or panelling, or paintings, as in the Elysium and Heaven Rooms. Behind the keep is a little enclosed garden, with a Venus fountain of unknown origin, but possessing the same romantic quality.

Sir Charles Cavendish's son, Sir William, built the great range of buildings to the E called the Riding

BOLSOVER Castle: the Portico and the Keep

School; and after that the monumental terrace facing W. This is now open to the sky. It is a unique building, eleven bays in length, with great upright rectangular windows, punctuated by extraordinary near columnar shafts: steep steps lead down to the grass walk below. On the courtyard side this building is entered by a grand portico, baroque in feeling. The whole atmosphere of Bolsover is magical.

The property descended to the Cavendish-Bentincks, Dukes of Portland, but was long ago given up as a place of residence. It is now admirably cared for by the Ministry of Public Building and Works.

Bolsover Church is chiefly of interest for its Cavendish monuments. The building was almost gutted by fire in 1897: the thirteenth-century broach spire and seventeenth-century Cavendish Chapel survived. There is a Norman S chancel door with tympanum, and a thirteenth-century sculpture of the Nativity. In the Cavendish Chapel are two magnifical monuments, one to Sir Charles Cavendish (d. 1617) with its remarkable euphuistic inscription, which makes use of an elaborate form of chiasmus; the other to Henry Cavendish, Duke of Newcastle (d. 1727).

Bonsall (8). An old lead-mining village in a valley behind Matlock: the cottages cling to the hillside, and the street winds up to the village cross (with thirteen circular steps), and the seventeenth-century King's Head Inn. The church stands even higher, with distinguished Perpendicular tower and spire, pinnacles and much decoration. Effective interior with clerestoried nave and elegant S arcade. Raised chancel with bright 1870-ish glass. Rood screen. Mediaeval slabs in S chapel. In the N aisle is a monument, with weeping cherubs and urns, to Henry Ferne of Snitterton Hall. Snitterton Hall, secluded in its back lane, is an enchanted late sixteenth- or early seventeenth-century manor house, with symmetrical gabled front, doorway with naive Ionic pilasters, and walled front garden with arched entrance.

There is a Baptist Chapel of 1824, and a Gothick Lodge on the way up from the Via Gellia. Everybody thinks at first that the Via Gellia is a Roman road. Not so; it is a spectacular craggy road, constructed in the eighteenth century by the Gell family of Hopton to give access to their quarries. "Viyella", the name of the brand of hosiery first made in a local mill, is a corruption of "Via Gellia".

Borrowash (5). Pronounced "Borrow-ash." In the suburban sprawl between Nottingham and Derby. Off the main road is the small brick church (by P. H. Currey, 1899). Inside there is a low eighteenth-century iron chancel screen, thought to be the work of Robert Bakewell. It was presented by the Pares family of Hopwell Hall.

BOLSOVER: the Colliery and the Castle

Boylestone (14). A little village in the undulating country S of Ashbourne. The church has a Victorian SW tower with pyramid roof; the rest is Victorianised mediaeval. Nineteenth-century roof. Victorian carved reredos. Ingenious tablet to Herbert Croft on N wall of nave, 1785.

Brackenfield (8). A good stretch of country, with the road N leading past the park of Ogston Hall and the great stretch of water, on and up to Ashover; the road W to the high ground towards Dethick. Small church with spire built in 1856. Monuments to the Turbutts of Ogston. Ancient screen removed from old church.

Bradbourne (11). A good position in the fine country NE of Ashbourne. A wide gravel sweep leads past a Victorian lamp-standard and the Old Parsonage to the church. Norman tower, with finely carved Norman doorway curiously set on S side of it. Saxon masonry on N side of nave. Fourteenth-century S arcade. Fourteenth-century chancel. In the interior High Church furnishings abound, and the good modern oak pews and pulpit, hanging lamps, altar ornaments and iron altar rails all owe something to the Arts and Crafts movement. There are old carved panels in the Lady Chapel screen, and the seventeenth-century painted text on the S wall by the door is a curiosity. Colourful Victorian E window; some old glass in sanctuary. Many monuments to Buckston family, including that of Thomas Buckston, "one of the oldest officers in H.M. Service" who died in 1811—he had fought at Culloden—and a pretty Gothick tablet to Mrs Ward of Sutton-on-the-Hill. In the churchyard is a Saxon cross, and to the E is the grey gabled Elizabethan Hall, with a beautiful garden and terrace to the N.

Some distance to the E of the village along the road to Hognaston are two stone farmhouses: one eighteenth century, the other a high gabled seventeenth-century house marked WB. IB. 1694.

Bradley (11). Narrow lanes lead to this hamlet. A Georgian Hall of somewhat undecided plan overlooks the little church, and water beyond. Well kept churchyard, with honesty and other flowers growing against the walls of the church, which is little more than a private chapel. Hatchment and monuments of the Meynells, who bought the place in 1655 from Sir Andrew Kniveton, who was ruined by the Civil War (see Mugginton). Large nineteenth-century tablet, with naval anchor, to an Archer who married a Meynell.

At Moorend there is an archway, known as the Hole in the Wall, across the road, with cottages attached; the road leads on to Bradley through the farmyard.

Bradwell (5). In the grand country between Tideswell and Hope. Samuel Fox, who invented the umbrella, was a native of Bradwell. The church

was built in 1868: of most interest are the early eighteenth-century furnishings—chancel screens, altar rails and so on—given to the church by the Revd R. B. Somerset, Fellow of Trinity College, Cambridge, and a native of the village: they must have come from some college chapel.

Brailsford (11). Main road village with brick cottages, one or two old farms, and an early nineteenth-century chapel with cast-iron Gothic windows. The church stands in fields, half a mile to the W, up a long drive. Sturdy Perp. tower; the body of the church largely Norman. Well-furnished interior with pleasant oak fittings and several good monuments. Across the fields it is possible to see Ednaston Manor, built by Sir Edwin Lutyens with all his characteristic charm.

Brampton (8). The village is largely intact, despite the approach of housing from Chesterfield's west end. Ashgate House, now a hospital, is a good tall Georgian stone house, with lunette windows. Opposite the church is the Hall, an old two-gabled house, with mullioned windows and stone-tiled roof, white-painted Gothic railing, and embattled garden door at the side. To the W of the church is an attractive school house, with simple front. The church has broach spire, and embattled clerestoried nave and chancel. Figures of SS Peter and Paul in outside wall of S aisle. Scraped interior, with de-varnished pine pews. Royal Arms of George III over chancel arch. Choir stalls erected in 1938 to the memory of Thomas Linacre of Linacre (1460–1524), Fellow of All Souls' and first President of the Royal College of Physicians. Thirteenth-century monument to Matilda le Caus, with effigy partly concealed by inscription. Large seventeenth-century tablet to Clarke family of Somersall, with strange Latin elegiacs —the final pentameter concluding in Greek! Grand monument to Sir Godfrey Clarke, Jacobite; and small inscriptions to the Gorell Barnes family of Ashgate.

Linacre Reservoir in the valley to the N is invisible from the church.

Brassington (11). The scenery is famous: the road to the village from the A524 passes the Brassington rocks, and the Harborough rocks are to the E towards Wirksworth. The church stands against the hill, overlooking the stone cottages, the narrow streets and alleys of the village. Norman tower: Victorianised Norman interior. Grand S arcade, Norman; N arcade Victorian Romanesque, with carved capitals on grey alabaster columns. Norman porch, and ancient door. Beautiful low Norman S arcade in chancel: chancel enlarged by Victorians, who inserted E wheel window. Tiled sanctuary. Pitch-pine furnishings. 1806 Royal Arms under tower.

Breadsall (11). A large residential village now very close to Derby. The church has the strange distinction of having been burnt by suffragettes in 1914. It was beautifully restored by W. D. Caröe. Light and spacious interior. Handsome modern furnishings. Famous fourteenth-century alabaster pieta, discovered under the floor in 1877. Splendid W tower and spire (thirteenth-century) of great height and elegance.

Opposite the W end of the church is a fragment of the Tudor Old Hall. Breadsall Priory now appears as a castellated early nineteenth-century house: in the basement is an arch of the original Augustinian priory. The seventeenth-century house which replaced this is now largely engulfed by nineteenth-century work. It was the home of Erasmus Darwin.

Breaston (15). In the flat country close to where the Derwent joins the Trent, too near many main roads and railway lines, and, above all, too near Long Eaton. The village still survives. Thirteenth-century church with broach spire. Early eighteenth-century font.

At *Draycott* to the W is an enormous lace factory. A lane leads down to Church Wilne and the Trent.

Bretby (14). A straggle of new houses lines the main road from Burton to Ashby, and the National Coal Board's Central Engineering Establishment is close to the entrance to Bretby Park. The drive leads through the undulating but mutilated park to the great castellated house built by Sir Jeffry Wyatville for the 5th Earl of Chesterfield in 1813–15. On the E front two big circular towers at the angles frame the terrace, which faces a well-wooded valley: on the S front a grand gateway leads in to the courtyard, and the W side is composed of a lower Jacobean range, an appendage of the earlier house. Everywhere Gothick details mingle with Georgian features. But the interior is entirely classical, though this has been altered to adapt it for its use as an orthopaedic hospital.

Kip's view of the old house shows it as a great palace, perhaps French in inspiration, surrounded by exquisite gardens. Celia Fiennes, who came here in 1698, mentions four levels of sunken gardens, and a hydraulic clock which chimed the hours to the tune of Lilliburlero! It was built about 1630 by the 1st Earl, but the architect is unknown. The 4th Earl, author of the famous "Letters", lived principally in London and abroad, and rarely came to Bretby. The house was neglected; his cousin and successor commissioned Wyatville to rebuild. The Stanhope connection came to an end in 1915, and the house became a hospital in 1926.

The drive leads on to the tiny village: a little green, with a small church nearby rebuilt in 1878. The most interesting thing in it is the brass tablet to Disraeli, "the foremost man of his age": he was a frequent visitor to Bretby. To the SW of the church is Castle Field, full of prominent earthworks. Here stood the castle of the Segraves, Mowbrays and Berkeleys, pulled down by the first Stanhope to come to Bretby in 1610.

Brimington (9). Overgrown industrial village between Chesterfield and Staveley. Church built *c.* 1860. Spidery Gothic interior, recently effectively redecorated. First War Memorial in S aisle, a marble figure of Britannia.

To the NE stands Ringwood House, early nineteenth century with verandah and coupled Ionic columns. This was the home of the Markham family, local industrialists.

The Church, BRADBOURNE ▷

46

Charles Markham (b. 1823) married the daughter of Sir Joseph Paxton: his daughter, Violet Markham, C.H., was Paxton's biographer. It is now a club.

Brizlincote Hall (14). Stands in a prominent position close to Bretby, overlooking Burton-on-Trent. The house was built in 1714 by Philip, 2nd Earl of Chesterfield, for his son. It is dramatic in its position, and dramatic as a building. Apparently designed by the Earl himself, brick with stone quoins, pedimented doorways on both fronts, pedimented windows, hipped roof, the whole composition is crowned on four sides by great segmental pediments. The effect is striking—perhaps the finest small baroque house in England. The Earl died before its

completion, and his son never lived here. For a century it has been a farmhouse, and the interior is disappointing. But with its splendid façades, and the relics of old avenues and gate-piers, it has all the makings of early eighteenth-century magnificence, on a small scale.

Buxton (7). "Buxton", wrote Christopher Hobhouse, "is a delicious town, combining the intimacy of a mountain village, with the spaciousness of an eighteenth-century spa." And "the air of Buxton is like wine, and the driest in England".

The Romans, with their passion for baths, thoroughly appreciated it. Before the Reformation it was a place of pilgrimage for those who sought health; Elizabeth I sent her courtiers to recuperate at the "baynes

of Buckstones"; Mary Queen of Scots was brought here in the custody of Lord Shrewsbury.

It is due to the Cavendish family that the town was developed as a spa in the eighteenth century. In 1781 the 5th Duke of Devonshire employed John Carr to build the Crescent, the Square, and the Riding School: it was hoped that Buxton would rival Bath.

Buxton's greatest period was at the end of the nineteenth century: great hotels were built, the Pavilion and the Winter Garden followed, large houses appeared in the spacious tree-lined roads, famous actors performed at the Opera House, but this period was short-lived. The immense Empire Hotel (1906, by Thomas Garner) arrived too late on the scene, and after being empty for

BRIZLINCOTE HALL

The Opera House, BUXTON

many years was pulled down not long ago.

The upper town is the old market town: tucked away at one end of the High Street is the little old church of St Anne. It was built in 1625. It is little more than a long, low chapel, and the dominant feature of the interior (apart from beautiful High Church furnishings) is the succession of enormous tie beams only about ten feet from the ground.

The street descends into the new town: here are shops or hotels, sometimes adorned with cast-iron verandahs (e.g. the Grove Hotel). To the left facing St Anne's Cliff, with St Anne's Well at its foot, is John Carr's Crescent (1781). Giant Tuscan pilasters rise from a rusticated base—which takes the form of a delightful arcade, raised a few feet above street level: above is a metope frieze, with cornice and balustrade, crowned at the centre with the arms of the 5th Duke of Devonshire. Inside the E wing, on the first floor, is the Assembly Room, now sadly disused, a large handsome room decorated with giant Corinthian pilasters, and shallow apse at the end screened by Corinthian columns.

Round the corner to the W is the Square, also by Carr, plainer, but carrying on the idea of the arcade. Facing the Square are the Pavilion Gardens and the entrance to the Pavilion and the Winter Garden. These were built in 1871 (architect, Edward Milner of Sydenham), evidently inspired by the Crystal Palace. Next door stands the Opera House (by Frank Matcham, 1903), an Edwardian baroque building, with elaborate painted ceilings. Above all this stands the new parish church of St John Baptist (1811), a classical building with E and W porticos; Kempe glass. The church is usually ascribed to Wyatville, but according to Mr H. M. Colvin is by John White. Higher still is Carr's great Riding School. In 1880 this was converted into the Devonshire Hospital: the vast dome was built to cover the great circular courtyard which had been used for riding. The dome was designed by Henry Currey. Currey also built the magnifical Palace Hotel alongside (1868).

Alas, the beautiful little railway station with its symmetrical frontispiece has been half destroyed. Paxton is supposed to have advised on the distinguished glass and iron façade, which screened the two termini—one, the L.&N.W.R. to Manchester, the other the M.R. to Derby and London. The latter line is now closed.

St Peter's, Fairfield, is an attractive church of 1839: W gallery on iron pillars, and Royal Arms of V.R. Gothic Ten Commandments. Monument to William Dakin, "a merchant of the City of London who was instantaneously killed on his own premises by the explosion of a cellular steam cylinder". Christ Church, Burbage, is a building of 1860 by Currey: interior with wooden piers and arches. Holy Trinity, a former Proprietary Chapel, is also by Currey (1873): handsome tower.

Trees, gardens, parks abound: Cliff Gardens (opposite the Crescent) were laid out by Wyatville; the Park by Paxton.

At *Harpur Hill* to the S are enormous lime works, and a small early twentieth-century church, built in debased Victorian Gothic. On Grin Low stands the early nineteenth-century circular folly tower called Solomon's Temple.

Caldwell (17). Lost in the lanes of S Derbyshire, a village of old cottages and two large farmhouses. The Hall, now a country club, looks over a small park: plain eighteenth-century S front with handsome urns at the angles, lower late seventeenth-century W wing overlooking the entrance

forecourt, with pedimented centre and mullioned windows. Small over-restored Norman church: two roundels of ancient stained glass in W window. Late Victorian reredos and glass in sanctuary. Brass tables to Gresleys, baronets, of Drakelowe.

Calke (14). Wooded country near Melbourne: the road to this tiny village is a cul-de-sac, and the village is now protected by the new Staunton Harold Reservoir to the S, and by Calke Park to the N. Calke Abbey is a great and unknown early eighteenth-century stone mansion, standing in the middle of its large well-guarded park. It stands in a

hollow, on the site of an Augustinian priory, and was built by Sir John Harpur in 1703, to replace the house at Swarkeston. Grandly impressive front facing S, three storeys high, eleven bays wide, with projecting wings to the right and left, and almost equally impressive façades to the E and W. Giant Ionic pilasters. Well-detailed cornice. All this may be the work of Francis Smith of Warwick, or his brother William Smith. It is known that in 1727 James Gibbs designed, and Francis Smith built, the stone staircase up to the front door on the *piano nobile:* this was replaced in 1804 by William Wilkins, who added the Ionic portico and the

below and opposite The Crescent, BUXTON, 1781

balustrade. The finest rooms are on the first floor, and a great saloon occupies the centre of the S front. The stables behind the house were built in 1714–16 by a local man called William Gilks. The lodges at the Ticknall entrance are by Wilkins. The house is still the home of the Harpur-Crewes. It is not open to the public.

On a knoll in the park, facing the Abbey, is the small early nineteenth-century Gothic church, beautifully furnished in the taste of the time. Monuments to Harpur-Crewe family, notably one by Cheere, to Sir John Harpur, 3rd Bt (d. 1741).

Calow (9). Mining village on the high road from Chesterfield to Bolsover. The church with its tall broach spire of unmistakable Victorian lines was built in 1869 (architect: Rollinson of Chesterfield). Dark, beautifully furnished, atmospheric interior.

Carsington (11). Enchanted country between Ashbourne and Wirksworth. Attractive chapel—embattled, with Perp. windows, and "Re-edified 1648" on a sundial on S wall. W gallery with organ. Gell tablets and memorial windows. Many attractive furnishings: seventeenth-century font cover, panelling from box pews, Riddel posts, hymn board, plaster cast of St Paul by Woolmer, 1851, for St David's Cathedral, given by Jowett (Master of Balliol) to Philip Lyttelton Gell. Royal Arms, Queen Anne, 1706.

Castleton (4). Grand countryside: one of the centres for exploring the High Peak and the Peak caverns. Peveril Castle stands guard to the S, Mam Tor to the W. The village is full of shops selling postcards and souvenirs.

The Castle was originally built soon after the Conquest by William Peveril (to whom the land was granted by the Conqueror); the keep was built in 1176 by Henry II. Much remains of keep and curtain walling, though the castle has certainly been a ruin since the seventeenth century.

Most of the church is rebuilding of 1837, though the Norman chancel

◁ Peveril Castle, CASTLETON

arch remains, and the Perp. W tower. Inside it is attractive, with box pews, and in the vestry is a library of some 600 books, left by a previous incumbent.

The Castleton Caverns are weird and awe-inspiring. The most celebrated, the Devil's Hole, was designated one of the Seven Wonders of the Peak by Thomas Hobbes; the Speedwell Cavern is almost equally striking, with its enormous single chamber, and roar of rushing water; the Blue John Mine is three miles long and contains a type of spar called Blue John, which is now in short supply.

Catton Hall (17). An imposing, plain, brick house, in the wide valley of the Trent, very close to Staffordshire. It was built in 1742–3 for Christopher Horton by William Smith of Warwick. For fifty years or more, owing to a misunderstanding of the surviving plans and specifications, the design has been wrongly ascribed to James Gibbs. Gibbs was indeed involved, but not directly with the design as executed. The interior contains original plasterwork and other decorative fittings, and the windows command a view up and down the river. The Hortons came to Catton in 1405, and the property passed by an early nineteenth-century marriage to the Wilmots of Osmanston-by-Derby, and so to the present owner. Small S wing added by Sir T. G. Jackson in 1907.

Chapel-en-le-Frith (4) means "Chapel in the Forest"—the Forest of the High Peak. The chapel or church was originally built by the foresters, and to this day the freeholders of the parish are patrons of the living. Old houses line the approach to the church: this is a mediaeval building, consecrated in 1225, but the S aisle is a rebuilding externally of 1733, when the tower was also rebuilt in handsome Georgian style (George Platt of Rotherham, architect). Interior scraped. Box pews. Hatchments. Monuments.

The great Ferodo works to the E below were founded some sixty years ago by Herbert Frood, who started developing brake-lining materials in

CHATSWORTH ▷
p54 79′ Waterfall from Joseph Paxton's Aqueduct, 1839–40
p55 Thomas Archer's Cascade, 1702

his little workshop here. The factory now covers eighteen acres.

High on the moors, two miles W of the town, is Bradshaw Hall, once the home of the Bradshaw family (of Col. Bradshaw the regicide fame). Jacobean. Date 1620 on garden gateway. And one mile to the E the high road to Castleton (A625) looks down upon Ford Hall in the valley below: seventeenth–eighteenth century.

Charlesworth (17). The curious interest of Charlesworth is that the Congregational Chapel was more or less the parish church from the seventeenth century until the nineteenth: oddly, the R.C. ducal family of Norfolk (who owned Glossop) allowed this strange balance of power. The big chapel on the hill (rebuilt in 1797), with its large graveyard, still dominates the village. The parish church itself was built in 1849, cruciform and Gothic, with a big tower over the N transept. Views over the hills to great blocks of flats in Manchester suburbs.

Chatsworth (8). Something has already been said in the Introduction (pp. 24–32) about the history of Chatsworth: to appreciate this remarkable place it is essential to know a little about the Cavendish family, and above all to remember their descent from Bess. It is also important to remember, when comparing Chatsworth with other houses, that it is no mere country house: it is a palace. "When you enter the park", writes Mr James Lees-Milne, "you are overcome by the vast scale of the prospect before you. Chatsworth is, you feel, a principality rather than a country house, even measured by the noblest standards."

The house as we see it today is the work of three men: the 1st Duke of Devonshire built the main block: the 4th built the stables and the bridge: the 6th added the vast N. wing and the belvedere, and added much to the interior.

The 1st Duke built the S front first (1687–9), and his architect was William Talman. The E front was built next, and was completed by 1695, and again the architect was Talman. Thereupon Talman was dismissed. The W front was completed by 1706: it is the most decorative and spectacular as well as the most familiar façade, but its architect is unknown. It is now thought to be the work of the Duke himself, in conjunction with his mason, John Fitch. The N front was completed last (1707), and is almost certainly the work of Thomas Archer. His clever Baroque device of the elliptical bow was used to conceal the difficulty of aligning the longer W front with the shorter E. Archer also designed the great Cascade, and the Cascade House (1702).

The 4th Duke married the daughter of the great Palladian Earl of Burlington, so it is not surprising to find him employing the Palladian James Paine to build the stables (1762) and the bridge (1761), while Capability Brown landscaped the new approach and diverted the river. Paine also built a new service wing to the N and made a new entrance court on this side.

This N wing was swept away by Wyatville in 1820, when the new N wing was built (375 ft long) to contain the new reception rooms for the 6th Duke. Wyatville also refaced the E front, and altered Archer's N front. The house is now entered through Wyatville's monumental gateway into the N forecourt, and so into James Paine's entrance hall.

The state apartments as contrived by the 1st Duke are all on the upper floor of Talman's S front: the visitor approaches them via the painted hall, the chapel and the great staircase; perhaps this strange arrangement is an echo of Bess's state rooms at Hardwick, which are also on the second floor. They comprise the state bedroom, the state music room, the state drawing room, and the state dining room. They were decorated by Laguerre, Verrio and Ricard, and the wood carving is by Watson (see Heanor).

◁ CHATSWORTH
The south-west corner

They are not large rooms, but they are gorgeous. It was the 6th Duke who, wanting larger reception rooms, employed Wyatville to convert the old gallery into the library (90 ft long) in 1830, and to build a new dining room (in the N wing) in 1832. The sculpture gallery, the orangery and the theatre followed.

The treasures of Chatsworth are famous; what is more, it is a delightful house to visit, as it is possible to wander in one's own time through the rooms. Credit is due to the present Duke and Duchess, who have, since the war, and in spite of the difficulties of the time and the crippling effect of death duties, moved back into the house, and made it a home as well as a palace.

Chellaston (14). Suburban growth from Derby creeps on, making of Chellaston a featureless sprawl. But the place was famous in the middle ages and long after for its alabaster, which was used extensively all over this part of England for tombs and sculptured figures. Burton and Nottingham were the great centres for this art. In the centre of what remains of the old village is the church. W tower, rebuilt in nineteenth century. Fourteenth–fifteenth-century church. Norman font.

Chelmorton (7). Remote village in Peakland. At the entrance to the village is a Georgian stone farmhouse with Venetian windows: the church is at the extreme end, where the road peters out into the hills. Fine grouping of W spire and church against hillside, and enormous churchyard with graves climbing the hill. The stone-vaulted porch is a gallery of early sculptures and sepulchral slabs, and the interior is one of unsophisticated charm, with long raised chancel, broad S transept chapel, and much plain glass. The fourteenth-century stone screen (with later wooden upper part) and octagonal carved font are notable. Two beautiful eighteenth-century marble tablets in chancel.

Chesterfield (8). The crooked spire has become a kind of hallmark for the town. Chesterfield is an ancient borough, which has become increas-

The Chapel reredos, CHATSWORTH

ingly important as an industrial centre: collieries, iron foundries and other factories abound. Apart from the Parish Church little of great architectural importance survives: it is, however, a town of character.

The church is of grand size, and chiefly of the fourteenth century. The nave is of six bays, and the span of the transepts is 110 ft. It has many fine furnishings which give the church a powerful devotional atmosphere. The earliest part is the crossing: the four pillars of the central tower date from 1234, when this portion of the church was

dedicated. The tower and spire were added at the end of the century, and most of the church completed by 1360.

It is not known when the spire became crooked, nor how exactly it happened: probably, as a result of the heat of the sun the lead-covered timber tilted and bulged. The effect is heightened by the lead plates being laid in herringbone fashion, which seems to give the whole spire an exaggerated gruesome twist. The lean is 7 ft 6 in to the S, 7 ft 10 in to the SW, and 3 ft 2 in to the W.

The effect of the interior is very

rich: there is good Victorian stained glass by Warrington and Hardman, and much modern glass, by Sir Niniam Comper, Miss Alrich Rope, and Christoper Webb. The High Altar is under the central tower: the Rood above is by Temple Moore (1915). Norman font. Early sixteenth-century Processional Cross. Jacobean pulpit. Vista across S transept, with magnificent screen of 1500 shielding the Lady Chapel and Lesser Lady Chapel. The former contains a series of alabaster monuments of the Foljambe family—an exceptional collection of eight, ranging in date from 1510 to 1604, and all of distinguished workmanship. The alabaster altar is by Harold Gibbons (1936). The Lesser Lady Chapel has a polygonal E end.

As for the town, the names of old streets survive: Saltergate, Knife-smithgate, and so on. The latter was rebuilt in half-timbering between the wars. Saltergate contains one good late eighteenth-century terrace, and there are two eighteenth-century houses in the Market Place—though that is dominated by the big mid-nineteenth-century Market Hall, with

its odd tower, all in bright red brick. The Town Hall in Rosehill was built in 1938 (architects Bradshaw, Gass and Hope): it is a neo-Georgian building, a style at present out of fashion—but it will come into its own. The new Court House nearby is an extreme contrast. Also in Rosehill is the early nineteenth-century Independent Chapel. But the building of greatest charm is the Unitarian Chapel of 1694 in Elder Way. Its beautiful main façade is hidden from the street, and with its old graveyard around it is worth exploring.

Of the other churches of Chesterfield, Holy Trinity is of 1838 by Thomas Johnson, in Commissioners' type Gothic. It is chiefly of interest because George Stephenson worshipped here, and is buried in the chancel. Christ Church is a mid-Victorian building of 1869, and SS Augustines' an unusual basilica-type church of brick (1930) by H. L. Hicks. The R.C. church of the Annunciation is a building of some originality by Joseph Hansom: vista'd interior, and towered continental W end.

CHELMORTON ▷

To the NE is the suburb of *Whittington*. On the edge of open country stands St Bartholomew's (1896) by C. R. Rollinson, a friendly late-Victorian church with spire, and one noble late Georgian urn-topped tomb in the churchyard. Next to it is a somewhat decayed low seventeenth-century stone farmhouse. Lower down the village street stands Revolution House, formerly the Cock and Pynot Inn, where the 4th Earl of Devonshire plotted, with other noblemen, the downfall of James II in 1688. It is a museum, and belongs to the Corporation. Beyond Whittington is New Whittington, with a church of 1927 (St Barnabas).

Newbold, to the NW, is now a suburb, but was once a manor in its own right, and Chesterfield one of its hamlets. Behind the Nag's Head Inn in Barlow Road, is the old R.C. chapel of the Eyre family, now disused. It was granted by James II for Papist worship, but was sacked by Protestants in 1688. Norman tympanum over S doorway. A new

CHESTERFIELD

R.C. church has recently been built a hundred yards away. The parish church was built in 1887 as an aisleless nave and chancel. A very successful enlargement took place in 1957, when wide aisles were added—rather the treatment given to small aisleless churches in the middle ages. High altar at chancel step; chancel now Blessed Sacrament chapel. Attractive commemorative tiles round church, e.g. one to James Boston, "killed in Bolsover Colliery 1902 *aet.* 16, on the eve of his Confirmation".

To the W is *New Brampton*. Here is St Thomas' of 1832, a Commissioners' type church, by Woodhead and Hurst. Very wide, aisleless interior; well-furnished chancel with canopied stalls; highly decorated flat roof—a very effective church. To the SE the old village of *Hasland* is now incorporated in the borough; there is a mid-Victorian church of 1851, now somewhat removed from this huge suburb. And to the E of the railway, in a surprisingly rural setting, surrounded by its little park, stands Tapton House, a pleasant late Georgian block of *c.* 1800, and the home of George Stephenson.

Chinley (4). A residential district for commuters from Manchester. Chinley Chapel is a rare seventeenth-century Independent place of worship. It was built in 1667: from the outside, with its two storeys and domestic-looking mullioned windows, it might almost pass for a house; inside it is galleried and charmingly decorated.

There is an 1874 parish church at *Buxworth*, with a little chapel-of-ease (1907) at Chinley itself—but the great thing at Chinley is the sight of the wonderful railway viaducts. Here the lines from Sheffield, Manchester and Derby converged at Chinley Junction: the two lines from Derby, to Manchester and Sheffield, were carried on two long curving viaducts high above the valley, and the road far below. Although these two lines are closed, it is earnestly to be hoped that the viaducts may be left. They are one of the greatest monuments to Victorian Industrial England—and to the Midland Railway. To the motorist or pedestrian passing underneath the effect of them is crushing, breath-taking.

Church Broughton (14). Impressive church; unusual big W tower, with N staircase turret and diminutive spire. Spacious interior, chiefly fourteenth century. Very long chancel: sedilia and piscina in sanctuary. Norman font. At the back of the church there is an enormous Royal Arms of George IV (1827), which apparently cost £8 12s 7½d! Views to the N to mansion and chapel of Barton Blount.

Church Gresley (17). Church Gresley and Castle Gresley are all part of the vast mining area round Swadlincote. There are the usual long streets of drab houses. Nothing remains of the Castle: perhaps a small portion of the Norman priory is incorporated in the church, though most of this is of 1820. One fine monument to Sir Thomas Gresley, 2nd Bt (1699), and one or two hatchments keep alive the memory of the once great family who took their name from this place (see Drakelowe). The set of old stalls and miserere seats at the W end came from Drakelowe Hall, and may have originally come from Gresley Priory.

Linton, to the SW, is a subsidiary village: red brick Victorian church (1881) with small apse and big dormer windows.

Clay Cross (8). Small industrial town S of Chesterfield, bisected by the A61. Drab little houses and shops along the main road. Good church of 1851 by Stevens, with tall broach spire: dignified, well-furnished interior.

George Stephenson founded the Clay Cross Company in 1837. When he was building the North Midland Railway (from Derby to Chesterfield and Rotherham), and driving the famous Clay Cross Tunnel, he was impressed by the ample deposits of coal, and was determined to develop them, as well as to supply his own needs for the railway. Embattled Gothic entrance to the tunnel (1840).

Clifton (11). There was a small mediaeval chapel here, pulled down in 1750. The present church was built in 1845 by R. C. Carpenter. It is rather grand, though not large. Fine sanctuary. Mosaics. Good Victorian glass. Royal Arms of George V, 1926. The pretty road to

the SW descends through wooded country to the valley of the Dove, to the delights of Snelston and Norbury.

Clowne (6). Industrialised colliery village: long rows of glum cottages line the main road. But the old village church lies to the S and overlooks fields. Perp. tower. Norman nave. Georgian porch. Modern chancel.

Codnor (12). Industrial countryside near Ripley. On the higher ground to the E are the somewhat brittle remains of Codnor Castle, built in the thirteenth–fourteenth centuries by the Lords Grey of Codnor, subsequently owned by the Zouch family, who sold the property in 1634. The castle then fell into decay. In Codnor Park is the memorial to William Jessop, founder of the Butterley Works, and celebrated engineer. It takes the form of a great Tuscan column, enclosing a spiral staircase to a platform at the top—from which a good view was obtained. Alas, it is now declared unsafe. The church is of thin Gothic of 1843 (architect, Robert Barker), attractively furnished and whitened within. Modern font, and stone Calvary outside W door.

Coton-in-the-Elms (17). Few elms are apparent, but this small village is in a rural setting in the extreme S of the county. The little church with its elegant spire was built 1844–6 by Stevens. In the chancel is a tablet to Theodore Echalaz, "for more than 47 years Vicar of Coton, to whose zealous exertion the building of this church is mainly to be attributed". Cast-iron painted Royal Arms of the period, and wooden triple sedilia by the font.

Cressbrook (see Miller's Dale).

Creswell (6). The Creswell Colliery was started by the Bolsover Colliery Company in 1894, and the large village of miners' houses has sprung up since. The brick church was built in 1899, at the expense of the Duke of Portland; the tower was completed in 1927. Creswell Crags to the E of the village form a picturesque limestone gorge, the cliffs containing a series of caves which have been excavated since 1870. Valuable relics of early human and animal life have been discovered.

Crich (11). Pronounced "Crych". A large village high up on the hills E of Matlock. It has become a household word among tram-lovers for the Tramway Museum, opened here in 1959. On the cliff above is Crich Stand, where there has been a view tower (built originally by the Hurts of Alderwasley) since the eighteenth century. In 1922 this was replaced by a lighthouse with flashing beacon, built as a war memorial to the Sherwood Foresters.

The large church has a nave with two Norman arcades, Dec. chancel and spire, and Perp. clerestory added to the nave, embattled outside. When the chancel was built, the nave was lengthened by the addition of the two fourteenth-century E arches. Monuments to William de Wakebridge (d. 1369)—in N aisle—and to German Pole (d. 1588) and John Claye (1632) in chancel. At Wakebridge, to the NW, was a mediaeval manor (pulled down in 1771 by Peter Nightingale, a forbear of Florence), which descended by marriage to the Poles. Norman font. Stone gospellectern in sanctuary (cp. Taddington).

The Tramway Museum has been established in a disused quarry, where a quarry railway was originally built by the Stephensons. Members of the Tramway Museum Society have laid the lines, erected the overhead wires, and restored the trams themselves. Trams have come from Sheffield, Southampton, Glasgow, Cheltenham, Blackpool, even from Oporto, Johannesburg and Prague. There are open-top trams, closed-top trams, single-decker trams, trams with balconies: there is a Sheffield tram of 1874, and one from Leeds of 1953. Members of the public can go for a longish ride through the old quarry; at present there is nearly a mile of track, and it is being extended. It is hoped eventually to build a small industrial town street, with re-erected Victorian buildings or shop fronts, at some point on the journey, under the direction of Mr Roderick Gradidge, the architect.

CHINLEY
above The Viaducts
below The Chapel, 1667

Cromford (8). Here in 1772 Sir Richard Arkwright established his first cotton mill worked by water: it is holy ground to the industrial archaeologist. Arkwright was born in Lancashire in 1732, and after developing early spinning machinery as a young man, came to Nottingham in 1768, and established there a cotton mill driven by horse power. In 1771 he came to Cromford, determining to use the water power from the River Derwent for a new cotton mill. This lowered the cost of production, and revolutionised the whole industry. The Cromford mill was the precursor of the hundreds of mills all over the N of England and elsewhere, upon which much of the wealth of Victorian England was built.

Cromford itself lies in a beautiful valley: there is a mediaeval bridge over the Derwent, with fifteenth-century chapel attached. Nearby stands the eighteenth-century Fishing Pavilion (inscribed "Piscatoribus Sacrum"). The old mill still stands close to the bridge, and is now used as a factory for dyes. The Bonsall Brook (a tributary of the Derwent) supplied the power, aided by water from the Cromford Sough (a seventeenth–eighteenth-century artificial channel used to drain neighbouring lead mines). Close to the Canal Basin are overgrown wharves and storage buildings; the canal itself was built by William Jessop of the Butterley Works at the very end of the eighteenth century. Here too was the terminus of the High Peak Railway, which connected Cromford with Whaley Bridge, New Mills and Manchester.

Up the main road to Matlock stand the Masson Mills (1783): the original building with its Venetian windows is now wedged between later additions, but is clearly identi-fied. Alas, that it has recently lost its little cupola and weather vane. Is it too much to hope that this may be replaced?

To the W of the Matlock road, near the entrance to the Via Gellia, is the centre of the village, with its grand late eighteenth-century Grey-hound Inn, built by Arkwright; and stone cottages built for the workers climb the hill westwards. North Street leads off at right angles—a kind of model industrial village, of 1777, with three-storeyed terrace cottages (the lofts were for hand-loom weaving) leading up to the school at the end.

On a fine site overlooking the river stands Willersley Castle, built for Arkwright in 1782–8 by William Thomas of London, a classical house in a Gothic dress. Below stands the church, built by Arkwright in 1797, and gothicised in 1857. Comfortable Victorian interior: polished

Bentley Hall, GREAT CUBLEY

oak, polished brass lamp standards in pews, brass lectern, mosaics in apse, walls covered with wall paintings and stencil work by A. O. Hemming, who also did the glass. Many Arkwright inscriptions—most notably: "In memory of Sir Richard Arkwright, Knight, Founder of this Church. Born at Preston in the County of Lancaster 1732. Died at Cromford 1792".

Further to the E stands the Railway Station (1860), probably designed by Paxton's son-in-law, G. H. Stokes—with its little pavilion on the up platform, its station-master's house on the hillside above, and its cast-iron footbridge, attractive and romantic.

Great Cubley (11). Green, undulating countryside, S of Ashbourne. Attractive church, which climbs the hill towards the eighteenth-century brick rectory to the E. Handsome late Perp. W tower, carved with many coats of arms of the Montgomery family: the big W window floods the nave with light, as do the large seventeenth-century windows of the nave. Lofty interior, with raised chancel. Fragments of mediaeval glass. Good Victorian E window. Alabaster tomb to Sir Nicholas Montgomery (1494) and other monuments. Traces of painting on chancel arch and E nave arcade.

Dr Johnson's father was a native of Cubley, and went from here to become a bookseller at Lichfield, where Samuel Johnson was born.

A mile to the E along the road to Alkmonton is Bentley Hall, an intriguing house. The E wing is late sixteenth or early seventeenth century, brick with stone quoins, with central bay window on first floor, supported on stone pillars. At right angles to this is an imposing late seventeenth-century wing, also in brick, with sash windows, and distinguished stone centrepiece framed by giant pilasters with handsome scrolled and pedimented architrave. It is now a farmhouse, and its presence here, close to the road, is mysterious.

Curbar (5). There is a small church of 1868, built by Salvin; but the most notable building is Calver Mill (1803), which rises over the river here, like a great six-storeyed warehouse near Tower Bridge. There is also an old village lock-up, a little square house with an ingenious conical roof.

Stoke Hall, nearby, is an elegant stone house of 1757, with two fine

Walter Evans' School at DARLEY ABBEY, 1827

fronts, and handsome stables across the main road, built for, and perhaps designed by, Mr Booth of Stoney Middleton (q.v.)—or even perhaps by James Paine himself.

Dalbury (14). A by-road near Sutton-on-the-Hill is sign-posted "Dalbury only"—a hopeful sign. Endearing little backwater. Small ancient church, with one mediaeval window of St Michael.

Dale Abbey (15). Little survives of the Abbey of Premonstratensian Canons, founded here in this secluded spot in the twelfth century. The E end of the church, with its great empty window, stands in the grassy field, and there is a small museum formed from what remains of the chapter house, on the E side of what was the cloister.

A short distance away is the parish church—half church, half house. It was originally the infirmary chapel. Its interior is of great interest, arranged still as it was in 1634, the date of the pulpit which stands

behind the little altar with its accompanying reading desk and clerk's pew. The altar itself, a seventeenth-century table with cupboards built in in the eighteenth, becomes a storage place for the sacred vessels. The chapel is a sea of box pews, extending into the aisle and overflowing into the little gallery at the W end. The whole is a rare and delightful survival.

The Dale Abbey property came into the hands of the Stanhope family after the Reformation, and there is a tablet on the N wall to "The Rt. Hon. Philip Henry, Earl Stanhope, of Chevening in Kent, Lord of this manor and Lay Bishop of this church, died March 2nd 1855. Erected by Parishioners." There are also traces of mediaeval wall paintings (e.g. the Visitation on N wall), restored by Professor Tristram in 1931.

There are one or two good houses in the village. On the sandy hillside, carved out of the cliff, is the Hermit's Cave, formed here, according to the old story, by the pious Derby baker

who in the twelfth century under the guidance of the Virgin gave up all his possessions and retired to this cave. Nearer the main road stands the Cat and Fiddle Windmill, still in working order.

Darley Abbey (14). An industrial feudal village, not far from the centre of Derby, but remarkably unspoiled and intimate. The Augustinian Abbey (founded in the twelfth century) was dissolved in 1539. All that survives is the low stone building in Darley Street, perhaps a guest-house or a barn. In 1783 Walter Evans built his cotton mill on the river here, and the Evans family presided in patriarchal style until 1928, caring for the village, and providing a kind of private "welfare state" of their own. Walter Evans built the church in 1819, the school in 1827, and rows of little late-Georgian cottages for the workers, who were well looked after by the family. The church is very late Gothic, by Moses Wood of Nottingham, and contains interesting monuments. The school is a distinguished two-storey, pedimented, Georgian building. Darley House, the home of the Evans family (but built 1727), was pulled down in 1962. The grounds are now a public park. It is possible to drive across the river by the toll bridge which adjoins the mill.

Darley Dale (8). Rows of rather gloomy Victorian cottages line the main road: at one end stands the grimly impressive Whitworth Institute, founded by the benefaction of Sir Joseph Whitworth, the engineer who invented "standard" screws, drills and gauges. There are club rooms and a library, playing fields, tennis courts, a lake—all that workers in local industries could want. Many beautiful Victorian details inside, such as the ironwork of the staircase. The architect seems unrecorded.

The old village stands to the W, off the main road, and here is the church. This is chiefly of the thirteenth and fourteenth centuries, but there are many twelfth- and thirteenth-century sepulchral stones built into the outside wall. Shaft of Saxon Cross. Wide, cruciform interior, dark, with colourful nineteenth-century glass: one window by Burne Jones (S transept), other glass (N aisle) by Powell. Mediaeval stone parclose screen in S aisle (contained Sir Joseph Whitworth's pew). Fourteenth-century tomb of Sir John de Darley in nave, and sixteenth-century Millward monument in sanctuary. Elegant little Greensmith tablet (eighteenth century) near lectern. Famous yew tree in churchyard.

Stancliffe Hall, on the rising ground to the E, was Sir Joseph Whitworth's house: E. M. Barrie greatly enlarged the earlier building. It is now a prep school. The former lodge (on the main road) is like a tiny French chateau. St Elphin's, the girls' public school, whose prominent buildings are near the main road, was originally built as hydro.

At S Darley (or Wensley) is a very comely neo-Norman church of 1843, by Weightman and Hadfield.

Denby (12). A village close to collieries. Denby pottery, first established in the early nineteenth century. The church has a broach spire, vaulted S porch, and Transitional-Norman S arcade. By a curious arrangement the N arcade was removed in 1838, and replaced by a gallery. Monuments to the Lowes and Drury-Lowes of Locko include a large alabaster tomb to Patrick Lowe (1616) and his wife, a Harpur of Swarkeston. Many modern furnishings, including a new pulpit of 1965, to replace that brought here from the chapel at Locko—now restored to its original home.

Denby Old Hall to the W of the church is now a farmhouse, dating from the sixteenth–seventeenth centuries. It was the original home of the Lowes.

Derby (14). Old prints of Derby of the eighteenth—and even of the nineteenth—century show the town as a market town, neat and compact, on the west side of the River Derwent.

Handyside's Great Northern Railway bridge at DERBY, 1878

The river rushes down its weir; there are the big houses of the merchants, and the town houses of the gentry: John Lombe's silk mill is prominent in the foreground; there are the towers of the mediaeval churches: St Alkmund's and St Michael's and St Werburgh's to the north, St Peter's to the south, and dominating the whole scene is the great tower of All Saints as the centre of the picture.

To the visitor today, approaching from the E, the scene is still recognisably the same. The big eighteenth-century houses are gone, but a portion of the old silk mill, rebuilt after a fire in the nineteenth century, is still there, and the river still rushes down its weir. The tall spire of St Alkmund's, rebuilt by Stevens in 1846, has only lately been destroyed to make way for the new road, and Gilbert Scott's great blackened spire of St Andrew's (1881) to the S is now being destroyed also, faint twentieth-century hearts having decreed the structure conveniently unsafe. Taller town buildings obscure the other old churches, but the early nineteenth-century spire of Christ Church is visible on rising ground behind, and the scene is still dominated by the great tower of All Saints, now the Cathedral. To the N stands eighteenth-century St Mary's Bridge with its mediaeval chapel alongside: the new Exeter Bridge, built in 1929 (architect, C. H. Aslin) leads into the Market Place, past the Council Offices on the left (also by Aslin), fine in conception, but disappointing in design.

The Romans had a station at Little Chester, now marked by the broad green close to St Paul's Church to the N of St Mary's Bridge. The Saxon coffin of St Alkmund was discovered during the excavations under St Alkmund's Church, and is now in the museum. But Derby's great historical moment came in 1745, when the Young Pretender arrived on December 4th, held a council of war all through the 5th, and retreated on the 6th, having (it is said) heard Mass in All Saints. Industry first came to the town in the eighteenth century with the opening of John Lombe's Silk Mill

DERBY Cathedral

in 1717. Lombe had smuggled himself into the silk mills of Italy and surreptitiously learnt the secrets which he brought back to England. Here on the banks of the Derwent he opened the first silk mill in the country, powered by the water of the river. He died a few years later, poisoned apparently by a jealous Italian agent. In 1783 Walter Evans opened the mill at Darley Abbey (q.v.) a mile or so upstream. But it was not till 1840 that the coming of the railway began the transformation of Derby into the great industrial town that we see today. The Rolls-Royce factory was established in 1907, and during the first half of the twentieth century it grew enormously. There are acres of drab Victorian streets, and even vaster acres of twentieth-century housing estates in the sprawling suburbs.

The best way to see Derby is to start in the Market Place, attractive in its rather formless way. On the S side stands the Town Hall (by Habershon, 1841), which replaced the eighteenth-century building which appears in old pictures. The shell of the Assembly Rooms is on the E side, sadly burnt in 1963; it is greatly to be hoped that this may be rebuilt. At present its fate hangs in the balance. There are several eighteenth-century houses adjoining the Town Hall, and on the W side of the square; to the N Irongate leads up to the Cathedral. Here there are two Victorian buildings worth noting: Westminster Bank House, a nineteenth-century town palazzo on the left, and the Derbyshire Building Society, in a kind of Florentine Gothic on the right; there are also a few old shops, such as Haslam's with its plastered gables, and Monkhouse the chemist, opposite the Cathedral. At the corner of Sadlergate, Lloyds Bank has a simple distinguished early eighteenth-century façade, and down Sadlergate itself are two seventeenth-century buildings, the Old Bell, and No. 48 with a baroque doorcase, sash windows on the first floor and wooden mullions and transomes above.

The tower of the Cathedral was built in the earliest years of the sixteenth century, and next to Boston

DERBY Cathedral

Stump it is the tallest mediaeval tower in England. The church itself was rebuilt by James Gibbs in 1723–5. It was raised to Cathedral rank in 1927. Do not expect a great mediaeval cathedral, for such it never was and never can be. It is one of the best eighteenth-century town churches in the country, and as such it cannot disappoint. It bears a distinct family likeness to St Martin-in-the-Fields, with its Tuscan columns and wide plaster vault. The organ is in the gallery at the W end, and Robert Bakewell's chancel screen is a superb piece of work, with the screens that divide the choir from the N and S aisles added in the nineteenth century. Around the walls, and especially in the Cavendish (S) Chapel are monuments, among them the tomb of Bess of Hardwick (1607), Rysbrack's to Caroline Cavendish, Countess of Bessborough (1760), the Earl of Bessborough (1793) by Nollekens, Thomas Chambers and his wife by Roubiliac (1735), and Richard Bateman by Chantrey (1821). Sebastian Comper's new chancel was begun in 1967 and is not yet complete. What it will add to the building we cannot tell till the present E wall is removed, and the new vista revealed. It is built in strict harmony with Gibbs' work, and promises well.

Past the Cathedral is the little St Michael's, rebuilt by Stevens in 1858, and beyond the site of St Alkmund's, where the new road rushes by below, is the R.C. church of St Mary. This was built by Pugin in 1838: with its lofty tower, its narrow nave with clerestory carried on slender tall arcade, its vaulted apsidal chancel and brilliant glass by Warrington, it is one of the most moving of all Gothic Revival churches. Nearby, in Well St., is Alkmund's Well.

The new road leads down to St Mary's Bridge (rebuilt 1788): beside it stands the mediaeval chapel of St Mary, restored to use in 1931, and adjoining it Bridge Chapel House (seventeenth–eighteenth century), the residence of a Canon of the Cathedral. To the S at this spot a new bridge is shortly to be built. In King Street, which is the continuation of Queen Street, and Irongate are two buildings of note, The Seven Stars (1680), and the old building

of Derby School, St Helen's House, with its stone Palladian front (mid eighteenth century).

Retracing our steps to the Cathedral and turning down St Mary's Gate we find several Georgian houses, and the County Hall, a most interesting building of 1660. Standing back from the street across a forecourt, the balustraded façade is composed of three big arched windows, and a pair of ornate baroque doorways set between them. The street leads on through Cheapside into Wardwick. Here there is one seventeenth-century building, the gabled Jacobean Café, and, opposite, the Library and Museum, in a brand of Flemish Gothic (by Knill Freeman, 1878). The Museum contains an interesting exhibit of the Midland Railway, and collections of pictures by Joseph Wright, and of china from the Crown Derby factory. To the right of the front are Bakewell's gates which once formed the entrance to John Lombe's silk mill.

Wardwick continues to the N.W. as Friargate. Here is St Werburgh's, where Dr Johnson was married in 1735. The tower is Gothic survival of 1601; the big new church was built in 1895 by Sir Arthur Blomfield, but the interesting chancel of 1699 remains, with contemporary woodwork and furnishings, now used as a side chapel. A little further on, again on the right-hand side, is Robert Ward's famous picture shop, where for generations pictures from most of the great collections in the Midlands have been restored. The street is crossed by the elegant traceried cast-iron railway bridge of the Great Northern (by Handyside, 1878) and beyond are the finest Georgian houses in the town, a long terrace of mansions and smaller houses, which give some idea of the style and scale of eighteenth-century Derby. Friargate continues as Ashbourne Road, and here and in Vernon Street are pleasant stuccoed Regency houses: at the far end of Vernon Street is the imposing Doric front of the former gaol, now dedicated to greyhounds. Almost opposite the turning into Vernon Street is Bridge Street, which contains St John's, built by Goodwin in 1828—Perp. style, with four grand angle-turrets, à la King's Chapel.

To the S of the Market Place Cornmarket leads into St Peter's Street, past the blackened fourteenth-century St Peter's, the only mediaeval church to survive (the tower was carefully rebuilt in 1898). In the churchyard alongside Robert Bakewell is supposed to have had his shop. St Peter's Street leads into London Road (to the left) and Osmaston Road (to the right)—and the great Victorian growth of the town is before you. In London Road is the Derbyshire Royal Infirmary, with a statue of Florence Nightingale outside. Further on, down Midland Road, is the Midland Station. Alas! Francis Thompson's famous Trijunct Station has been ruined, but fragments survive of its former glory. The Midland was always proud of its provincial character: even after St Pancras was built, Derby was always the headquarters, and it is worth standing outside the imposing façade, with its attendant office buildings and the hotel opposite. Nearby is the Company's war memorial, and the garden which was the directors' tennis court, where the directors could besport themselves after a board meeting. By contrast, further down London Road, is the new B.R. Research Centre (1964)—a spacious and imposing design by Dr F. S. Curtis, chief architect at B.R. H.Q., which has already won a Civic Trust award.

Down Osmaston Road is the old workhouse—now the factory of the Royal Crown Derby Porcelain Co. Crown Derby china was first made by André Planche (of Huguenot descent) in about 1750, and Planche was joined by William Duesbury I, and a factory founded soon after in Nottingham Road (near St Mary's Bridge), where a house now bears a commemorative plaque. This factory was closed in 1848, when a small new factory was opened in King Street by men from the Nottingham Road works. Meantime, in 1878, the Osmaston Road factory was started, and in 1935 the King Street factory merged with this. There is a good museum here, containing a collection of Crown Derby china from 1750 to the present day, representing the work of all the famous Crown Derby

St Werburgh's, DERBY ▷

names: William Duesbury I and William Duesbury II, Michael Kean, Robert Bloor.

Almost behind the Crown Derby Works is the Arboretum, laid out by J. C. Loudoun in 1840. In the gardens is a statue of Sir Henry Royce; and not far away, in Nightingale Road, is the Rolls-Royce factory, founded in 1907, and planned by Sir Henry Royce himself. Since 1945 the motor-car division has been moved to Crewe, but it was in the Derby factory that all the famous early "Silver Ghosts" were made.

The other churches of Derby are as follows:

St Anne's, Whitecross Street (1871). Perhaps the most attractive church in the town: a plain brick exterior with bell turret, the interior rich and lofty with all the intimate devotional atmosphere of a Tractarian place of worship.

St Augustine's, Upper Dale Road (1897), by Naylor and Sale. Late-Victorian red brick: rather grand interior with raised chancel.

St Barnabas', Radbourne Street (1880), by A. Coke Hill. Contains unique eighth-century cruciform font, traditionally used for recusant baptisms at West Hallam by Saint Edmund Campion.

St Bartholomew's, Nightingale Road (1927), by Curry and Thomson, the architects of Kelham Chapel. Recent extensions (1966) by Hurst, of Humphreys & Hurst of London.

Christ Church, Normanton Road (1839), by Habershon. Commissioners' type Gothic.

St Chad's, Mill Hill (1882). Plenty of polished oak and marble.

Holy Trinity, London Road (1904). Redolent of its date and district.

St James', Malcolm Street (1867), by J. Peacock. A vintage Victorian interior.

St Luke's, Parliament Street (1872), by F. J. Robinson. A tremendous Victorian tour de force, with saddleback tower 140 ft high.

St Mark's, Francis Street, Nottingham Road (1938), by Bernard Widdows.

St Osmond's, London Road (1904), by P. H. Currey. An elegant interior.

St Paul's, Mansfield Road (1849), by Barry and Brown. A homely, village-like church.

St Thomas', Pear Tree Road

(1883), by J. Peacock. "Norman": rich interior with glittering mosaics and large marble font.

Suburbs:

St Edmund's, Allenton, by Eaton of Derby, 1939; restrained 1930s Gothic.

St Edmund's, Allestree; the old village church, richly Victorianised by F. J. Robinson, 1866. Memorials to the Mundys of Markeaton Hall, and the Evans of Allestree Hall.

St Nicholas', Allestree: a friendly brick church of 1957.

St Mary's, Boulton; one Norman doorway, but the church rebuilt in the nineteenth century, and again enlarged in the twentieth, by Sebastian Comper.

St Michael's, Alvaston. The old village church rebuilt in 1856. Saxon coffin lid.

St Mary's, Chaddesden. Noble fourteenth-century village church, now engulfed by housing estates. Wide nave and aisles, lofty chancel, fifteenth-century rood screen and stalls, stone sanctuary lectern, monuments to Wilmots, baronets of Chaddesden Hall (demolished after first world war).

St Philip's, Chaddesden. An economy church of the post-war era (1953).

St Peter's, Littleover. Victorianised village church, further enlarged since the war by Sebastian Comper. One Norman door at W end. Monument to Sir Richard Harpur (1635).

St Francis', Mackworth. A simple housing-estate church of 1953, bright and airy.

St John's, Mickleover. "Contemporary" design of 1963, by G. J. W. Thomas, in memory of Bishop Rawlinson.

St Giles', Normanton. A mid-nineteenth-century rebuilding of an ancient chapelry. Norman tympanum.

Derby is well supplied with public parks: Allestree (to the N) contains a golf course; Markeaton has lost its mid-eighteenth-century house (the home of the Mundys) since the war, but the park is watered by the Markeaton Brook, here made into a lake; to the S is the park of Osmaston.

Prints survive of this elegant eighteenth-century mansion, the home of

the Wilmot-Hortons (see Catton), which fell a victim to industry. The family is commemorated in the neighbouring suburb of Wilmorton.

Dethick (8). In a lonely and wonderful position stand great farm buildings, an enormous sixteenth-century barn, and a chapel with ornate Perp. tower. This was the site of the grand mansion of the Babington family (see Ashover), who married the heiress of the Dethick family in the reign of Henry V. The Chapel itself is thirteenth century: it is narrow and lofty. In 1532 Sir Anthony Babington added the elaborate tower —it is decorated with a grand display of heraldic shields showing the family connections of the Babingtons.

Anthony Babington of the Babington plot was great grandson of Sir Anthony. He wisely made over Dethick, before becoming involved in the plot, to his brother George, but he was a spendthrift, and the place passed into other hands. All that survives of the original house is the great barn.

Dinting (1). Adjacent to Glossop: the main road to the NW leads to Manchester, by the blackened Holy Trinity Church (1875) with its tall spire. But all is dwarfed by the great Dinting Viaduct, which carries the railway from Sheffield to Manchester. This line was opened in 1845 by the Sheffield, Ashton & Manchester Railway, and the original Woodhead Tunnel (of ill repute) was at that time the longest that had yet been built: it was just over three miles in length. Dinting Viaduct is 120 ft high. Impressive landscape of desolate moors and industrial valleys. (See also Hadfield.)

Dovedale (10). The W frontier of Derbyshire. From Hartington to Ashbourne is nine miles as the crow flies; the river should unquestionably be walked every yard from Hartington to Thorpe, about seven miles. It cannot be seen except by walking, for the road only crosses it once. Here the Dove runs down a valley, almost a gorge, of steadily increasing beauty and grandeur. Towards the end the river is flowing at 500-ft level, while the sides of the valley shoot up to over a thousand. "The limestone

70

formations on either side are of inexhaustible variety, sometimes grotesque, sometimes terrifying, and sometimes exquisitely lovely", wrote Christopher Hobhouse; "in May and June they are covered with a riotous exhibition of ferns." And "the river itself is a perfect foil to the grandiose display of rock; it flows rapid, shallow, and silver-clear, through the heart of the tremendous defile it has made for itself, like a young princess between two ranks of grey-haired ministers and soldiers bowing as she passes".

Dove Holes (4). Bleak country of lime works and moors N of Buxton. Dreary village street of workers' houses, a chapel, and small Victorian Gothic church. Dove Holes tunnel was the longest tunnel on the old Midland line to Manchester, built in 1865, and nearly two miles in length. The Bull Ring is a prehistoric circle. The wide ditch and two entrances remain: all the stones were pilfered in the eighteenth century.

Doveridge (13). The village looks W across the River Dove into Staffordshire, and Uttoxeter is opposite. The Hall stood in a good position close to the church: this was built in 1769 by Edward Stevens (pupil of Sir William Chambers) for Sir Henry Cavendish Bt, later created Lord Waterpark, of an illegitimate branch of the Cavendish family. The house was pulled down in 1951; garden walls survive, and new houses have been built in the grounds.

The church has a very wide nave and chancel (early English) with no chancel arch—which increases the impression of space. Perp. tower and spire and clerestory. Many monuments to Cavendishes and others—notably the one to Sir Thomas Milward, the Royalist (1658), with angels holding back curtains from the inscription. Incised alabaster monument to Ralph Okeover and his wife (1390). In the churchyard an ancient yew of some eminence.

Between Doveridge and Sudbury stands Brocksford Hall, built in 1893 (John Douglas, architect), a restrained but romantic late-Victorian house, now a prep school.

Drakelowe (17). The ancient family of Gresley lived at Drakelowe for eight hundred years; their house has been demolished, and on its site stands the largest power-station in Europe.

The manor of Drakelowe was first held by a forbear of the family, Nigel de Stafford, in 1086, the Gresleys subsequently taking the name of the neighbouring village of Gresley. They were prominent in local affairs through the Wars of the Roses, the Reformation, and the Civil War: Sir George Gresley was one of the first baronets, so created in 1611.

Drakelowe Hall, originally an Elizabethan house, was largely re-built in 1723 by the 4th Bt, and Tudorised in 1830 by the 8th. The most famous feature was the Painted Room, now in the Victoria and Albert Museum. This room was painted in the eighteenth century with a continuous landscape, to create the illusion of a woodland glade. The cornice was replaced by a coved ceiling, so that trees and hills appeared to run up into the open sky above, the fireplace was disguised as a grotto, and all round real trellis-work took the place of a dado. In 1902 Sir Reginald Blomfield laid out terrace gardens leading down to the River Trent.

All through the nineteenth century portions of the great estate were being sold off; finally Drakelowe itself was sold in 1933, so breaking a link that had survived through twenty-eight generations. The house was pulled down in 1934.

In 1948 the site and nearly 750 acres were compulsorily purchased by the British Electricity Authority. Drakelowe "A" station was completed in 1955, "B" in 1960, "C" in 1966. There are eleven enormous cooling towers.

Dronfield (5). The main railway line to Sheffield and the A61 run through the narrow valley, and the old town clings to the hillside on the W. It is now in the middle of coal and iron industries, and being so close to Sheffield is almost engulfed by "development". The church with its tall spire dominates the town: it is large and handsome with lofty Dec. chancel. Ancient stalls. Jacobean pulpit. Brasses to Fanshawe family and other interesting memorials. The odd tracery in the large Dec. E window is seventeenth century.

In the streets round the church are several good houses, such as the Manor House (now Council Offices), and the Grammar School Headmaster's House (1731). Henry Fanshawe founded the school in 1568 (see Holmesfield). Gothic Town Cross (1848) in front of the Manor House commemorates the repeal of the Corn Laws.

Duffield (11). A large village on the A6, with a number of good Georgian houses on the main street—including the pretty little Baptist Chapel of 1830. Duffield Hall has a Jacobean core, but was much enlarged in 1870. It is now St Ronan's School for girls. The church stands by itself, near the river and railway. Fourteenth-century tower and spire. Interior comfortable and Victorianised. Tomb to Sir Roger Mynors (of the Herefordshire family), died 1536; he had property at Windley in this parish. Unusual monument (with acrostic inscription) to Anthony Bradshaw.

Nothing remains of the once great Norman castle of Duffield. The site, on Castle Hill, was excavated in 1886: the keep was of enormous size.

On Chevin Hill is a tall square tower—George Stephenson's "Sighting Tower", built on a line with the railway and the tunnel (1839).

Earl Sterndale (7). The by-road, off the main Ashbourne–Buxton road, that leads to Earl Sterndale passes through some of the most dramatic and beautiful scenery in Peakland. It looks perfection in snow, when the low winter sun creates wonderful blue shadows under the strangely shaped cliffs and hilltops, and there are wide views across further cliffs and hills into Staffordshire.

Remote little village: an inn called the Quiet Woman, and a small early nineteenth-century Gothic church which had the odd distinction of being the only church to be bombed in Derbyshire during the war. Restored and refurnished in 1952.

Little Eaton (11). Spreading village on the A61, not far from Derby suburbia: a wide green, and a church apparently Victorian-Norman. There was an ancient chapel, which in the eighteenth century was used as a blacksmith's shop. A modest new church built in 1791, which was enlarged in 1837: this in turn was swamped by the new "Norman" aisles, chancel and tower, built in 1851. Views across the Derwent to the hills behind Duffield.

Long Eaton (15). The small village of Long Eaton grew into the industrial town within a hundred years: lace works, silk works, railway works, bicycle works—all have added to the great suburban sprawl that surrounds the low Trentside between Nottingham and Derby. There is little of note in the centre of the town. The original Norman church of nave, chancel and W tower became the S aisle of the new church built by G. E. Street in 1868. Sir Charles Nicholson built the church of St John in 1916; only the nave has been completed. It is in brick with stone dressings, and attractive in its details, such as the beautiful leaded lights in the big plain glass windows. Trent College was founded in 1866, under the aegis of the Wright family of the Butterley Company, as an Evangelical Public School—a reply, as it were, to Nathaniel Woodard's High Church foundations. The nucleus of the buildings is of the late 1860s and early '70s, by F. J. Robinson of Derby. The chapel was rehabilitated in 1949 by Sir Albert Richardson.

Eckington (6). Large colliery village, with streets of Victorian miners' houses and shops. Impressive series of chapels on the road that climbs to Chesterfield. Renishaw Park is an oasis to the E. Interesting church: plain exterior with Norman tower, rich interior with Norman arcade and Perp. clerestory; S aisle and porch eighteenth century. Many Sitwell monuments, especially to George and his wife, the first Sitwells to come to Renishaw, in 1625. He founded the Renishaw Ironworks, and so re-established his fortune, nearly lost in the Civil War. Also unusual monument to Sir Sitwell Sitwell, the 1st Bt (d. 1811), in the form of a Corinthian column surmounted by an urn. Altar picture ascribed to Caracci, brought back from Spain by Sir Sitwell.

Fine Georgian rectory opposite the church (c. 1795).

Edale (4). Narrow lanes lead off the main road near Castleton and reach Edale vale. All around is the grand forbidding country of the Peak—Kinder Scout to the N, Mam Tor to the S, Brown Knoll to the W. A small collection of houses makes up Edale village: there is a little Victorian church of 1886. A remote spot.

Edensor (8). The village of Edensor (pronounced Ensor) was moved to its present site in 1839: previously it was uncomfortably close to Chatsworth House. The new village was planned and laid out by Sir Joseph Paxton, the ducal gardener, and the houses were mostly designed by John Robertson of Derby, and are intentionally fanciful and exotic: barge boards, "Norman" windows, "Elizabethan" chimneys, castellations abound. The scheme was crowned by Sir Gilbert Scott's grand new church (1869), and its tall spire provides an important feature of the landscape. Large monument to Henry and William Cavendish (d. 1616 and 1625), the two elder sons of Bess of Hardwick, the latter the 1st Earl of Devonshire. This is attributed by Mrs Esdaile to Maximilian Colt. The epitath on William is delightful: "Laboris ac Fidei capacissimus, Actu otiosis simillimus"—"he was capable of the utmost diligence and of unsullied faith, with the appearance of the greatest indolence".

Edlaston (11). Remote little village in beautiful lanes S of Ashbourne. Edlaston Hall, now a farmhouse, is a tall, early eighteenth-century house, brick with stone quoins, with a great central chimney. It sits quietly dominating the adjoining farm buildings.

The little church is mainly fourteenth century, with pretty double bell turret of 1900. 1815 sundial on S side. Cast-iron Royal Arms in porch.

Egginton (14). The Every Arms is a landmark on the main road from Derby to Burton: the village lies on a by-road half a mile to the W. The Every family, baronets, have lived here since the sixteenth century, but

the Hall (by Samuel Wyatt, c. 1780) was pulled down after military occupation in the war. It had some family resemblance to other Samuel Wyatt houses (like Hurstmonceux Place) with its domed central bow. Sir John Every lives in the Dower House (concealed by high brick walls) called Cothay, after the manor house in Somerset, whence the Everys came to Egginton. The 1st baronet, Sir Simon (1641), was a distinguished Cavalier. Many modern houses have been built behind the Park wall.

The little church has a low tower, and a chancel with roof steeply pitched above the levels of the nave. Hatchments and monuments to the Everys. Ancient stained glass in E window. Interesting map near door made by the present baronet showing all the fields in the parish marked with their ancient names.

Monks' Bridge is the mediaeval bridge over the Dove: the dual carriageway is conveyed on the new bridge alongside. Nearby the Trent and Mersey Canal is carried over the Dove on the long aqueduct built by James Brindley in 1777.

Elmton (9). Tiny rural village not far from the colliery settlement of Creswell. Church rebuilt 1773. Simple Georgian building with low unfinished tower. Pulpit with sounding board: portrait in the vestry of Jedidiah Buxton, illiterate labourer and arithmetical genius.

Elton (8). Peakland village with several good eighteenth-century stone houses, mostly slightly decayed. Plain church of 1812, a simple Georgian building dressed up with a few Gothic details: battlemented W tower. Nice Royal Arms of George III in vestry. The mediaeval church was destroyed by the collapse of the spire in 1805.

Elvaston (15). Elvaston has been for years a secret oasis, bounded on three sides by the suburban growth of Alvaston, Spondon and Borrowash: castle and church are almost invisible from the outside world—the outside world, even Spondon

Houses in EDENSOR, ▷
Chatsworth's Model
Village, 1839

ELVASTON Castle

Power Station, is completely invisible from castle and church.

The property came to the Stanhope family in 1539: Sir John Stanhope of Elvaston (d. 1610) had a son Philip by his first marriage who was created Earl of Chesterfield (see Bretby), and a son John by his second marriage who was founder of the Elvaston branch, Earls of Harrington. The Earls of Harrington remained in possession here till 1964.

The castle was designed by James Wyatt in 1812, and built after his death by Robert Walker, who added the stucco wings and tower to the W. The E front is by Lewis Cottingham, and portions of the seventeenth–eighteenth-century house are incorporated in this large castellated ensemble, for instance the E wing on the S front, and corresponding interiors. The painted hall, romantic and colourful, is by Walker: there are other more restrained Gothic or Classical rooms also. The greater glory is the formal garden laid out by the 4th Earl, with elaborate topiary work, the whole approached by the Golden Gates to the S. There is a temple in the Moorish taste. The park has ample plantations, lake and grotto.

The Dec. church is impressive and full of interest: Perp. W tower, chancel enlarged in characteristic splendour by Bodley (1905). Many fine tombs, especially to Sir John Stanhope (1610) in the chancel; a second Sir John (1638) in white marble, peering eagerly from his half-recumbent position—the tomb was restored by his grandson in 1731, after damage by Sir John Gell in the Civil War; Charles, 3rd Earl (1829), on N wall of Nave—"Charles 3rd Earl of Harrington lies here entombed with his ancestors"—by Canova; Algernon Stanhope (1847), aged nine, recumbent effigy in chancel by Westmacott; and the 5th Earl (1862), a recumbent effigy in Stanhope pew. A Perp. screen surrounds this family pew (E end of S aisle): there is seventeenth-century woodwork within.

The Elvaston Castle estate has now (1969) been purchased jointly by the Derbyshire County Council and Derby Corporation, to form a county park, an open estate of 390 acres in the midst of suburbia. The castle itself is to be a museum, information centre and restaurant—the grounds to be used for caravan-camping, riding and other sports,

and nature study. It is now open to the public.

Etwall (14). Chiefly famous as the birthplace of Sir John Port, founder of Repton School (q.v.). He also founded the Etwall Hospital. Port died in 1557: the Hospital, or Almshouse, was rebuilt in 1681, and comprises three sides of an open courtyard facing the N side of the church: there is a fine centrepiece, with scrolled pediment and coat of arms. Etwall Hall was a splendid moderate-sized early eighteenth-century house, with distinguished stone balustraded S front, with little end pavilions in the Palladian manner, and wrought-iron gates by Robert Bakewell. Sadly, it has been demolished since the war and replaced by the vast John Port Grammar School. The house stood on the site of Port's own mansion.

The church stands above the busy main road, and appears outwardly a building of the Perp. period. Inside the N arcade is Norman, and the N aisle forms the chapel of the Hospital, with carved stalls for the inmates. On the S side of the chancel stands the canopied tomb of Sir John Port, late Gothic in design, with brasses of Port himself and his wife and daughters above the tomb.

Eyam (5). Pronounced "Eem". Renowned as the "plague village". The infection was apparently brought to Eyam in 1665 in a box of clothes sent from London to the village tailor, and some 250 of the 350 inhabitants died in the course of a few months. William Mompesson the rector, and Thomas Stanley, the recently ejected Nonconformist minister, with the greatest devotion continued to look after their flocks. Mrs Mompesson died, and is buried in the churchyard. "Plague Cottages" are in the main street near the church.

Notable Saxon cross in churchyard, carved with Christian symbols and interlaced scrollwork: one of the very few crosses of its date to preserve its head and arms. Church much restored in nineteenth century.

Norman font. Eighteenth-century pulpit. Mompesson's chair, 1665.

Eyam Hall, with its gateway to the street and its half-H plan, little gables and mullioned windows, looks Jacobean, but is in fact dated 1676: it is one of the best of the smaller seventeenth-century manor houses in which the county abounds.

Nearer the church is the handsome Georgian rectory.

Fenny Bentley (11). The Bentley Brook runs down into the River Dove, joining the Bradbourne Brook on the way. Fenny Bentley is the first village on the grand road from Ashbourne to Buxton; the scenery is still intimate and enclosed: steep lanes lead up to Thorpe, and the wonders of Dovedale beyond. The church was much restored in the middle of the nineteenth century; it is attractive and full of interest. Notable early sixteenth-century

traceried screen with canopy—reminiscent of the Devon screens. Fourteenth-century chest. Monuments to Beresfords—particularly the strange shrouded figures of Thomas Beresford and his wife (1473). He was the first Beresford of Fenny Bentley, and fought at Agincourt. The old fortified manor house of the Beresfords stands opposite: square mediaeval tower, with gabled house attached, now a farm. Charles Cotton's mother was a Beresford, and he and Izaak Walton often came here.

Findern (14). There is some dormitory growth from Derby, but the old village green survives: the tall chimneys and cooling towers of Willington Power Station peer over the higher ground from the Trentside to the S. The church was rebuilt in 1863, and has a stumpy broach spire. Built into the N aisle wall is

EYAM Hall

the Norman tympanum from the earlier church, and an alabaster slab to Isabella de Fynderne (d. 1444) also survives. The Fyndernes were a powerful mediaeval family, whose name crops up in local history all over S Derbyshire: their heiress married Sir Richard Harpur of Swarkeston. Octagonal font of 1666.

Foolow (5). High Peak hamlet close to Eyam. Magnificent, desolate country of stone walls and rolling hills. The cross on the small green has an ancient base.

Foremark (14). Foremark Hall is the prep school for Repton. It is a distinguished stone Palladian country house, built *c.* 1760 for Sir Robert Burdett, 4th Bt, by David Hiorne of Warwick. The main rooms are on the piano nobile: on the entrance (N) front there is a central pedimented Ionic portico, and on both N and S fronts the canted bay windows are surmounted by domes—not unlike Isaac Ware's Wrotham Park (Middx),

built in 1754. The interior, complete with marble chimney pieces, plaster and woodwork, is well cared for by the school. The Burdetts were an interesting family, and included Sir Francis, 7th Bt, Champion of Liberty (d. 1844): they also owned Ramsbury Manor, the seventeenth-century John Webb house in Wiltshire, which they acquired by marriage in the eighteenth century. After the last war, on the extinction of the family, Foremark was taken over by Repton School.

There is no village of Foremark, but on the edge of the Hall grounds is the church, which at first sight appears Perp., but was in fact built by Sir Francis Burdett, 2nd Bt, in 1662. It is an interesting example of seventeenth-century Gothic survival. The interior contains original furnishings—box pews, three-decker pulpit, chancel screen, wrought-iron altar rails (by Robert Bakewell), carved wood and marble altar, and many monuments and hatchments.

At Ingleby nearby is the so-called

Anchor Church—caves cut out of the escarpment of the Trent, traditionally an anchorite's cell, but romanticised by the Burdetts.

Glossop (1). The famous Snake Pass descends into the town, and there is country of high desolate moors all round. The town grew during the nineteenth century on cotton and calico, and wears a grim manufacturing aspect. Old Glossop lies to the NE, around the parish church. New Glossop, or Howard's Town, is the modern centre, with its Town Hall of 1838. For centuries it was the property of the Howards, Dukes of Norfolk, and there is a considerable R.C. population. Above the entrance to the Railway Station stands a great lion, the Howards' crest. Glossop Hall (1850) has been pulled down since the war: the grounds have become a public park. The parish church nearby was largely rebuilt in the early nineteenth century, and again in 1914 (Charles Hadfield, architect). Tower and spire

FOREMARK Church, 1662

The Long Gallery, HADDON HALL

1853: one mediaeval arch (NE chapel). It is now a large building of atmosphere, filled with beautiful Anglo-Catholic furnishings. Old cottages round the church. Nearby, on the edge of the moors, stands the grand, severe neo-Grecian R.C. church (by Weightman and Hadfield, 1836). Great pedimented front with Tuscan pilasters.

St James', Whitfield, is a characteristic church of 1849, and St Mary's R.C. Church is a building of great magnificence of 1887. Soon after, to the S, the town peters out, and the road climbs on to the moors again. On high ground to the NW is Melandra Castle, which was a Roman station and fort: the site has been excavated.

Grindleford (5). Superb country. To the N are the Longshaw Moors (National Trust), and to the NW where the A625 climbs Millstone Edge is the great panorama known as The Surprise. To the E along this road is the Fox House Inn (seventeenth century), which is identified as Whitecross in *Jane Eyre*. After the opening of the railway (Totley Tunnel is dated 1893), Grindleford became a resort for Sheffield: there are many late-Victorian and Edwardian villas. The church was designed on a grand new scale by Sutton and Gregory in 1901: an imposing chancel and S chapel were built—but no more. The previous little aisleless church serves as a very modest nave—a strange but not unpleasing effect within.

Across the station bridge (opposite the Maynard Arms), and over the old water mill, a lane leads along the side of the railway to *Padley*.

Here are foundations of the old manor house of the Eyres and Fitzherberts. All that survives is the S range which formed the gatehouse, and, above, the chapel. Sir Thomas Fitzherbert of Norbury (q.v.), who married the heiress of the Eyres, was a devout Roman Catholic at the worst time of the Elizabethan persecutions. Two famous priests, Nicholas Garlick and Robert Ludlam, were arrested here in 1588, and subsequently hanged, drawn and quartered by St Mary's Bridge in Derby. Thomas Fitzherbert died in the Tower of London in 1591, his brother John in the Fleet Prison in 1598. The family finally sold Padley in 1657; all that survived of the house was the chapel, by then a cowshed. In 1933 this was purchased by the R.C. diocese of Nottingham, and restored. The original stone altar

77

was recovered from the ruins, memorial windows inserted; much of the original hammerbeam roof (with supporting angels) survives. It is a place of pilgrimage for Roman Catholics in the summer.

Haddon Hall (8). Haddon is the ideal mediaeval castle-cum-manor house. It is remarkable for its romantic beauty, remarkable for its natural position, remarkable for its preservation, most remarkable of all for being the genuine thing, untouched by the "improvers" of the eighteenth century or the "restorers" of the nineteenth. Its survival is due to its having been abandoned, like other early houses, such as Compton Wynyates, for 200 years, all through the eighteenth and nineteenth centuries.

There is early work here of the twelfth and thirteenth centuries, but most of what we see is of the fourteenth and fifteenth: the Entrance Tower is of 1530, and the Long Gallery wing was added by Sir John Manners, and completed in 1597.

The Entrance Tower leads into the Lower Courtyard: on the south side is the Chapel: on the the east the cross-wing which divides Upper from Lower Courtyard. This contains another tower, with archway into the Upper Court via the Screens Passage—the Great Hall opening off to the right, the kitchens and offices to the left. Other living rooms lie beyond the Hall—the Parlour, the Solar, the Earl's Apartments, all containing much original decoration —and so to the Long Gallery, the finest room in the house. This is shorter and lower than the Gallery at Hardwick, and therefore entirely different: it is lit by windows on both sides and at the end, so is light and intimate, but sumptuously panelled: over the fireplace is Rex Whistler's painting of the house (1933).

Like everything else at Haddon, the Chapel is a miracle of survival. There is ancient woodwork: screen, pews, three-decker pulpit; ancient glass in the east window; and mediaeval wall paintings of St

◁ HADDON HALL

Mediaeval painting ▷
in the Chapel

Christopher. Everything at Haddon is a tribute to the learned and gentle restoration of the house by the 9th Duke of Rutland, which was completed in 1927. It was his life's work.

See also the Introduction (p. 32).

Hadfield (1). Close to Glossop. Turreted Victorian church (1874). The only old house is the Old Hall (1646), now sadly derelict. Recently opened Railway Centre (adjacent to Dinting station) contains railway relics, and is regularly open to the public. (See also Dinting.)

West Hallam (12). Still a good village, but threatened by suburban growth from Ilkeston. The church is in a good position overlooking the valley to the S. The Great War memorial at the gates is a period piece. The church is chiefly fourteenth century. Pretty Victorian stained glass in chancel. Elizabethan tomb to Walter Powtrell and his wife, with well-preserved effigies: she was a Shirley of Staunton Harold.

Handley (6). A chapelry of Staveley, but intact as a small rural village. Small but attractive aiseless Victorian church. Intimate, beautifully furnished interior. Apsidal sanctuary with fine altar ornaments, and W gallery.

On the way up from Staveley stands Hagge Farm, a tall symmetrical gabled house of 1630.

Hardwick Hall (9). Hardwick is a very strange house, but also very beautiful—one of the most beautiful houses in England. It is strange for its six great towers, which beckon the traveller from far and near, for its enormous windows, which grow in size as the house soars upwards, for its grandest rooms being placed on the top floor, for its great stone staircase, which wanders up to those splendid rooms. Its strangeness is due to its remarkable builder.

Something has been said in the Introduction about Bess of Hardwick. She began this house in 1590 towards the end of her life, when she was seventy and after her fourth husband had died. She finished it when she

◁ Bas reliefs on either side ▷ of the Presence Chamber on the top floor of HARDWICK HALL

F

was seventy-seven, and she lived for another ten years after that. Hardwick had been her childhood home, and the old house of her family lies almost next to her new house—in ruins—a strange garden ornament indeed.

Walk through the park with its stag-headed oaks, look up at the towers from the lower ground to the W, approach its long garden wall, turn in at the little gatehouse, and the great façade, "more glass than wall", is upon you. "It's a house of moods, Sir," said the porter at the gate; and indeed it is. Sometimes this W front shimmers in the sunshine; more often, it seems, it stands glum against a louring sky, and the blackened stone takes on the hue of coal from the local collieries.

The low entrance, through the Tuscan colonnade, is strange also—giving into a Great Hall of unexpected height and lightness. To the right a passage leads to the staircase "which winds inconsequently through the house like a long passage", as Mr Nigel Nicolson has remarked: "a discursive staircase", according to Mr Christopher Hussey. This leads to the Dowager Duchess' Drawing Room, finally to the High Great Presence Chamber on the floor above. Sir Sacheverell Sitwell has called this "the most beautiful room, not in England alone, but in the whole of Europe". Next door, on the E side of the house, is the Long Gallery, lit by twenty of the tallest windows, hung (like all the house) with tapestry, and containing at least a hundred Elizabethan and Stuart portraits. The tapestries part, and a tiny doorway leads into the Green Velvet Room, and other bedrooms, and down again to the Chapel and the Dining Room. Everywhere there is rush matting, everywhere tapestries, stone floors, alabaster chimneypieces, elaborate stucco ornament. Walk through the garden—to the herbaceous borders against the stone walls, to the herb garden, to the long yew alleys on an axis with the S tower. The house casts its strange magic spell. The designer may have been Robert Smythson: the creative genius must have been Bess herself (see also pp. 24–32).

HARDWICK HALL

82

Roman Catholic Church, HASSOP, 1816

Hassop (8). Mysterious and unexpected. The severe Classical Roman Catholic Church, with its five big Grecian windows and Tuscan pilasters, rises above the road in the centre of this small hamlet. The W portico, like the front of a Grecian temple, faces the tall gate piers of the Hall. A mid-nineteenth-century Tudor gazebo stands alongside, and through the iron gates long walls, fifteen feet high, line the approach to the old home of the Eyres.

The Eyre family came to Hassop in the late fifteenth century, a younger branch of the Eyres of Padley (q.v.) Throughout penal times this fervent R.C. family often sheltered Papist priests in the house: when times improved they were able to build their church outside their gates—in 1816. The architect was Joseph Ireland. Handsome interior with coffered ceiling, baroque altarpiece with *Crucifixion* by Lodovico Caracci, and monument to Thomas Eyre, the founder, by J. E. Carew of Brighton.

The present house, probably incorporating an earlier building, was originally built by Rowland Eyre in the early seventeenth century: there is a blocked mullioned window and plaster overmantel of this period in an upper room. But the house now appears as a late Georgian rectangular balustraded building of three storeys, with four canted bay windows and central doorcase facing S. There are early nineteenth-century interiors, with plasterwork, and chimneypieces by White Watson (of Ashford-in-the-Water). To the N of the house, against the steep hillside, are the stables, and the great ballroom, built in 1833 by Thomas Eyre, approached by a vaulted passage and stairway, which also leads to the terrace garden.

This intriguing place continued to be the home of the Eyres, and their successors the Leslies, till the early years of this century. It is now the home of Sir Francis and Lady Stephenson, who have done much to preserve the house, and recreate the interesting garden, which is open to the public on certain occasions in the summer.

Below the Hall, and close to the road to Bakewell, is the late seventeenth-century gabled Dower House.

Hartington (7). Small town, beloved of anglers and walkers, close to Dovedale and Beresford Dale. The road from the S leads down past the Hall, a gabled manor house of 1611, now a Youth Hostel, but formerly home of generations of Batemans, whose memorials are in Derby Cathedral, as well as in the church here. Diminutive market square, with Town Hall of 1836, and numerous eighteenth- and nineteenth-century stone houses and cottages.

The church stands above the town to the N, an attractive composition of the thirteenth and fourteenth centuries, cruciform and battlemented, with a perpendicular west tower.

S of the town in Beresford Dale is the little seventeenth-century fishing house built by Charles Cotton, and frequented by him and Izaak Walton.

Hartshorne (17). Suburban growth from Woodville draws nearer, but in the centre of the village are the half-timbered manor house and the church. This has a fifteenth-century tower, and a body of 1835, with cast-iron tracery in the windows which will appeal to lovers of early nineteenth-century Gothic. The interior is attractive: W gallery on delicate cast-iron columns, and alabaster tomb near the W door of Humphrey Dethick and his wife (1599), with well-preserved figures.

Hathersage (5). Close to the Yorkshire border, and to moorland: Stannage Edge is behind. Hathersage is the Morton of *Jane Eyre*. Charlotte Brontë knew the village well, and often stayed at the vicarage.

The church is above the village, and the general appearance is Perp.: battlemented tower and spire, clerestoried nave. The bones of the fourteenth-century building are, however, apparent within. The NE chapel was the Eyre chantry, added in 1463. The church is famous for the Eyre brasses: there are four of the fifteenth and sixteenth centuries, and two of the seventeenth. The Kempe glass in the E window came from Derwent church—submerged under Ladybower Reservoir. Butterfield restored the church in 1852. Outside the S door is the grave of Little John—friend of Robin Hood.

A mile and a half to the NE, on the edge of the moors, stands North Lees Hall, a small rectangular tower house which Mr Mark Girouard associates with Robert Smythson. In the half-derelict ground-floor room is plasterwork dated 1596. It was the home of the Eyres—once so powerful in this part of Derbyshire—who also held another sixteenth-century manor house, Highlow Hall, a mile and a half to the SW. They were a Roman Catholic family, and their influence lingers on in the little early nineteenth-century classical R.C. church in the middle of the village.

Hayfield (4). A town of character, and a good centre for exploring the moors and Peak. Old cotton mills and factories: steep hills and narrow streets. Parish church of 1818: galleried interior with iron columns and box pews. To the N of the town stands Park Hall, screened by trees from the main road. It is a Grecian house of 1811; the crescent-shaped stables are really finer than the house itself.

Hazlewood (11). Favoured residential district on high ground between Belper and Duffield. Small church of 1840 by Stevens, largely built by the Colvilles, to whom there are memorials.

At North Lees Hall near HATHERSAGE ▽

Heage (11). A big village on the hills above Ambergate, with views over industrial Ripley. The church is strange: there is the small mediaeval building facing E, to which a much bigger church facing N and S was added in 1836.

Morley Park Ironworks, to the SE, were established by Francis Hurt of Alderwasley (q.v.) towards the end of the eighteenth century. There is a splendid pair of stone furnaces, one built in 1810, one in 1818: dramatic square pyramids with flat tops, built against the side of the hill—standing grand but forlorn in their now oddly grassy surroundings. They are some of the most appealing of early industrial buildings.

Heanor (12). Industrial town close to the Notts border. Hosiery works, brickworks, collieries. The parish church has a Perp. W tower, but all the rest is of 1868. The most interesting thing in the building is the monument to Samuel Watson, the wood-carver at Chatsworth:

> Watson is gone, whose skilful art display'd
> To the very life whatever Nature made.
> View but his wondrous works at Chatsworth Hall
> Which were so gaz'd at and admir'd by all.

There are also some pretty monuments of the nineteenth century to the Miller-Mundy family of Shipley Hall, a house which has been pulled down, and the park overrun by collieries.

All Saints, Marlpool, on the main road into the town from the S is a late Victorian church of which only the tower survived a fire soon after the war. The church itself has been attractively rebuilt in a restrained twentieth-century Gothic by the architect Peter Wore of Derby.

St Andrew's, Langley Mill, to the NE is a church of great interest, built in Arts and Crafts Gothic, 1911–12. (Key at off-licence opposite —Home Ales.) Nearby are the large Aristoc and Morley factories.

St Luke's, Loscoe, to the NW is an attractive church, too, of 1936—a kind of aftermath of the Arts and Crafts Movement.

Heath (9). Good views to Bolsover.

It is possible, too, to look down on the M1, with its great network of fly-overs and under-passes. Church of 1853 by Stevens: hard rock-faced exterior, decent interior with clean lines and devotional atmosphere. Ancient slabs in porch, one with carved crucifix, which came from the old church, of which fragments may be seen a quarter of a mile down the hill. Large new school (Heath County Secondary School) in the village.

Hilton (14). Main road village. No church. Sixteenth-century timbered house, with symmetrical front and simple plaster ornamentation, built by the Wakelyn family.

Hognaston (11). A stone village with several old houses and cottages. The church has a Norman door with an incised tympanum which has a representation of a bishop with crook, surrounded by the Lamb of God and several weird beasts. The font is also Norman, and the tower thirteenth–fifteenth century. The rest of the church is Victorian: vistas of arcades with carved capitals in chancel and NE chapel.

Holbrook (11). On the high ground behind Belper, between the A6 and the A61. Georgian church, built in 1761 by Samuel Bradshaw, and apparently little more at first than a chapel for the Hall (the small Classical stone house of 1681, close by). In 1841 this was largely rebuilt, and further enlarged in the early twentieth century, with some Art Nouveau embellishments.

Holloway (8). Rhododendron country above the valley of the Derwent, SE of Cromford. Leahurst is the old home of Florence Nightingale; she was born at Florence, but this was her parents' home, where she spent some of her childhood—and where she returned after the Crimean war in order to escape the publicity of London. It is a seventeenth-century gabled house, to which her father added considerably in 1825. The house called Lea Wood is by Nesfield, built 1870–6, with much exotic decoration. Lea Hall is a grand, moderate-sized early Georgian house.

Christ Church was built by the Smedley family in 1903. It is perhaps

the finest of P. H. Currey's Derbyshire churches, built in Arts and Crafts Perp. style, with imposing central tower, lavishly decorated sanctuary, and excellent stained-glass and furnishings of its period.

Holmesfield (5). On the high and beautiful road to Totley Moor and the Peak District, with views over Sheffield to the N below: a paradise for walkers. The church is 1826 with big Georgian windows in the nave, and a more Gothic pinnacled W tower. The chancel was added in 1895, and enlarged in 1963. Gaily decorated interior; modern stained-glass.

Two pairs of seventeenth-century gate-piers lead to Fanshawe Gate Hall—the former home of the Fanshawes (see Dronfield)—the present house being but a fragment of the original mansion. Woodthrope Hall, a gabled house of 1636, was also a Fanshawe house, built from some of the materials of Fanshawe Gate. The gate-piers here came from Derwent Hall, when that village was flooded for the Ladybower Reservoir. A third house, Cartledge Hall, is an Elizabethan farmhouse, containing old panelling and plasterwork.

Hope (5). The beautiful Hope Valley stretches from Castleton to Hathersage. Main road village with distinguished church: Dec. broach spire; battlemented, clerestoried nave and S porch (with parvise room above) all Perp.; well-furnished interior, with panelling and stall backs in chancel made from sixteenth- or seventeenth-century box pews. Kempe glass in chancel; windows by F. C. Eden in Lady Chapel. Shaft of Saxon cross in churchyard.

A mile to the E, off the main road, is the hamlet of *Aston*. Small Elizabethan manor house of stone, with tall central gable, unusually decorated with three-light pedimented window, with carved figure in the pediment, and front door with Tuscan columns. High-walled garden and farm buildings.

Hopton (11). Green and craggy country near Wirksworth. Hopton Hall is an Elizabethan house, Georgianised in the eighteenth

HORSLEY

century. Gells have lived here since the fourteenth century. It was the home of Sir John Gell, Parliamentary General of the Civil War, and of Sir William Gell, classical scholar and traveller, friend of Byron and Scott. It is still the home of the family. For many years the House of Commons' mace was preserved in the house—given to Sir John Gell by Cromwell ("Remove this bauble"). There are other relics of Sir John still here. The S front was embellished in the eighteenth century with Venetian windows, and crowned with a segmental pediment. The garden to the E is bounded by a great brick serpentine wall, with a tall gazebo-tower in the centre. There is little village: along the road to Wirksworth are Sir Philip Gell's almshouses (1720), redbrick Sycamore Farm, with central bow and Venetian window, and a smaller stone house in between, with bow front and Gothick window—three delightful buildings.

Horsley (11) looks down on the unceasing traffic on the A61, and is an oasis between Derby suburbia and the industrial Erewash valley. Dis-

tinguished church, which appears spectacular when approached from the E. The all-embattled and pinnacled exterior is fifteenth century, the church itself fourteenth century. Broach spire. Wealth of mediaeval details. Spacious, light interior. Grand Perp. font and sedilia.

At *Kilburn* is a good early eighteenth-century gabled Hall, close to the village street, but well protected by a high wall.

Horsley Woodhouse is a large towny village, nearer industry and on the road to Heanor. Church (St Susanna) of 1882.

Hulland (11). Main road village between Ashbourne and Belper. Gothic church of 1851, with embattled tower, lofty nave and short chancel. Box pews, two-decker pulpit, W gallery, flat ceiling, hefty Victorian font, hatchment (Borough family). Close to the green, to the W, are two old brick houses: Hulland Hall has stables crowned with an elegant white-painted cupola.

Remote in lanes to the N (no through road) is the hamlet of Biggin. Early-Georgian Biggin House is small but imposing, with giant

Tuscan pilasters at the angles and a classical frieze.

Idridgehay (11). In the pretty valley that leads N to Wirksworth. Characteristic Victorian church with spire, by Stevens, 1854. A good seventeenth-century, pink-painted, timbered house called South Sitch, and the Black Swan, with Gothick windows, opposite. A mile to the N stands Alton Manor, a gabled, pinnacled, embattled, towered house by Sir Gilbert Scott, overlooking its lake and small Victorian park.

Ilkeston (12) is a hill town above the Erewash Valley. "A town singularly devoid of visual attractions", notes Dr Pevsner—but there is a certain grim attractiveness about the views over the great industrial sprawl that stretches all along this eastern frontier.

In the market place is the Town Hall, a modest Victorian baroque building in brick of 1868. Opposite, the parish church, of considerable size and interest. The W tower, originally rebuilt in 1723, but gothicised in 1854, was taken down in 1909, and rebuilt stone by stone further to the W, at the end of the three additional western bays which were then added to the nave. Of the original church, the three easternmost bays of the S arcade are of *c.* 1200: those of the N arcade are fourteenth century. The N chancel arcade, with delicate many-shafted piers, is of great beauty, as are the sedilia and piscina. Opposite these is the early fourteenth-century tomb of Sir William de Cantelupe, Lord of Ilkeston. The fourteenth-century stone chancel screen is a rare object indeed. The whole church was much restored by Walker in 1855.

There are two town churches by P. H. Currey: St John the Evangelist, 1894, and St Bartholomew, Hallam Fields, 1895—the latter with a saddleback NW tower, and both in brick, and a somewhat earlier church in stone (Holy Trinity, 1883). The R.C. church, dedicated to St Thomas of Hereford, (a member of the Cantelupe family) was completed in 1931; it has a little stone corona.

At Cotmanhay, to the N, is a small, stone, turreted church of 1847, by Stevens.

Ironville (12). Industrial village close to Notts, built by the Butterley Company in the mid-nineteenth century. Grand church of 1852, apsidal, with decorative W tower. Memorial windows to William Jessop, founder of the iron works.

Kedleston (11) is the latest in date of the four greatest houses of Derbyshire, having been built entirely in the mid-eighteenth century. But the Curzon family who built it, and happily still own it, have been at Kedleston for over 800 years. This is easily the longest tenure in the male line in Derbyshire, and one of the longest in England. Something of the family history is to be found in the Introduction (p. 35).

There was already a good late seventeenth-century house at Kedleston in 1758, when Sir Nathaniel Curzon, 5th baronet and 1st Lord Scarsdale, decided to rebuild. First he employed Matthew Brettingham, who was replaced in 1761 by James Paine: Brettingham had built the NE pavilion, but it is to Paine that we owe the great N front—the grand central block linked, in the Palladian manner, to two smaller pavilions by

curving arcades. But Robert Adam was soon called in: it was he who designed the domed S front, and decorated the whole of the interior.

The entrance portico leads directly into the Marble Hall on the piano nobile. This, with fluted Corinthian columns of pink alabaster (each one a monolith), and coved ceiling, is one of the most magnificent rooms in England. From it lead off the State Apartments in sequence: the Dining Room, the State Bedroom, the State Boudoir, the Library, the Drawing Room, the Music Room—with, in the centre of the S front, the domed Saloon. Each room is a masterpiece of Robert Adam's decorative skill: each room is still filled with the furniture designed for it. Some have been recently done up with skill and knowledge by the present Lord and Lady Scarsdale.

The old village was entirely swept away when the park was landscaped: the bridge across the Lake is by Adam (1761) and not far away are his boat house and bath house. Alone, the old church survives, behind the NW pavilion. The S door is Norman, but most of the building is thirteenth century: the central tower is Perp. It is filled with a remarkable sequence of family memorials, starting with Richard de Curzon and his wife (d. 1275), and ending with the sumptuous tomb to Marquis Curzon, Viceroy of India (d. 1925).

Killamarsh (6). Large industrialised village close to Sheffield. The church is in a by-street, hard to find. It is much Victorianised, but there is a Norman doorway, Perp. tower, and small fifteenth-century stained-glass window of the Virgin in the chancel. The ancient font bears strange scars on its top—where cobblers' knives were sharpened. Scene of long Victorian incumbency of F. J. Metcalfe, Tractarian pioneer in these parts.

King's Sterndale (7). Remote and lovely spot close to Ashwood Dale: cottages and larger houses set in gardens against backcloth of beechwoods. The road through the village peters out beyond the green. Little church by Bonomi, intimate and beautiful; Gothic, 1847. The "Queen Dowager" gave £20 to its erection—Queen Adelaide was then living in

Derbyshire, at Sudbury Hall. Brass to Ellen Hawkins "foundress of this church". Windows of Thomas More and George Herbert, and other memorials to Pickford family, including one to William Pickford, the Judge, Lord Sterndale (1923).

Kirk Hallam (12). Houses are creeping up the road from Ilkeston, but there is some village atmosphere round the church. This is a small, ancient, but somewhat Victorianised building. Perp. W tower. Norman font. Eighteenth-century altar rails.

Kirk Ireton (11). A comely village of stone houses, a short distance above the main road from Wirksworth to Duffield. At the W end of the street the Barley Mow is a tall seventeenth-century house with twin gables surmounted by ball finials. Next to the church is an eighteenth-century brick farmhouse. An eighteenth-century gateway from the manor house (long ago demolished) leads into the churchyard. The church is above average for details. Pinnacled tower with weather vane: small clerestoried nave, embattled chancel with S aisle. Perp. chancel arch with unusual capitals, and unusual ogee arches in chancel itself. Fourteenth-century doorway into sacristy, with thin shafts and ball flower ornaments.

Along a narrow lane to the SW is Blackwall, a small estate with an early nineteenth-century Tudor manor house close to the road, held by the Blackwall family since the fifteenth century.

Kirk Langley (11). Several attractive houses along the main road, especially the tall Georgian Meynell Arms. Meynell Langley Park is ancient, and has long been Meynell property, though it has twice gone out of the family, once in the Civil War, once by marriage. To an earlier hunting lodge Francis Goodwin built a new front in the early nineteenth century, in the restrained Grecian taste of the period. It is still the home of Meynells, and contains an interesting library. Mediaeval church, largely fourteenth century. Perp. tower. Well-

KEDLESTON ▷
above North front, James Paine
below South front, Robert Adam

KEDLESTON, the Marble Hall

furnished interior. Old tiles. Heraldic glass. Ancient screens. Monuments.

Kniveton (11). Stone village NE of Ashbourne. A great sycamore stands at the churchyard gate. Small thirteenth-century tower and diminutive spire. Simple interior with grained and varnished pews and W gallery. Georgianised windows. Some ancient glass in chancel. Rustic-grand eighteenth-century monument in nave to Greenwood Holmes, erected by a dutiful nephew.

Langwith (9). The road from Notts passes by slag-heaps and miners' cottages and under railway bridges— and suddenly a frontier sign announces DERBYSHIRE. There is one old stone house with gables and mullioned windows, now a farm, and at Upper Langwith the small, aisle-less, bell-turreted church. Sturdy late Perp. porch with vaulted roof and depressed four-centred arch. Norman door. Interior much renewed: one roundel of ancient glass, plain oak rood, and pulpit with panels of gilded Lin-crusta! In the vestry a tablet to Michael Hartshorne, who died *aet*. 14 in 1747: "amantissimus coniux et pater carissimus posuit."

Litton (see Tideswell).

Locko Park (15). One of the great surprises of Derbyshire is the exist-ence of Locko Park. It lies only two miles from Spondon, behind the sprawl which seems to stretch for so many ghastly miles from Derby towards Nottingham. But here is a great deer park, set suddenly in gentle undulating country, and in the heart of it, facing a wide lake, is the mansion of Locko.

Locko was, in mediaeval times, a leper hospital: at the end of the sixteenth century it was purchased by the family of Gilbert, who in turn sold it to the Fernes. In 1747 it was bought by John Lowe of Denby, and it is his descendant who lives here today.

The earliest part of the house is the chapel, built in 1669, but the main

90

block is a house of c. 1730, nine bays wide and three storeys high, with giant rusticated pilasters. The house was greatly enlarged c. 1850, in the Italianate style, with a tall tower behind, porch and dining room and, above all, a grand picture gallery. The house, and in particular the picture gallery, contains a collection of pictures of great interest, made in the nineteenth century by William Drury-Lowe. The park is private, and the house is not open to visitors.

Longford (14). Hall and church stand apart from the village in the park. The church is large and handsome, and has a Norman core; the Norman N arcade survives—the aisles and spacious chancel are fourteenth century. At the E end of the S aisle is an array of alabaster effigies of the Longford family, beginning with Sir Nicholas of 1357, and ending with another Sir Nicholas and his wife of 1610. Upon the death of the last Longford the property passed to Clement Coke, younger son of Sir Edward Coke, the Chief Justice, of the Holkham family—and there are a number of good eighteenth- and nineteenth-century marble monuments to Cokes: younger sons of the Holkham family seem to have inhabited Longford during these years. They were not related to their neighbours and namesakes, the Cokes of Trusley and Melbourne.

Longford Hall was originally a Tudor house: the long brick S front was remodelled about 1700, the triple Tudor chimneys breaking at intervals the line of fifteen sash windows. The interior of the house was largely rebuilt after a fire in 1942.

Long Lane (14). The odd name denotes a Roman road. Small scattered village, which includes Osleston and Thurvaston. Christ Church, Long Lane, of 1859 by Robert Evans, with the school of 1865 and the bell tower of 1875, makes a pleasant brick group. Unspoiled Victorian church interior.

Longstone (8). Village street, climbing gently up the hill with long narrow green to the village cross. Opposite is the gate to the Hall—a square brick house of 1747, with stone dressings and quoins, in a dignified setting of wide smooth lawns. Mediaeval

church, restored by Norman Shaw in 1873. Original roofs throughout, with carved bosses. Ancient screen at E end of S aisle forms the old chapel of the Eyres of Hassop. Brass to Roland Eyre and his wife (1624) which originally contained Catholic symbolism, removed soon afterwards by Protestant zeal.

Close to *Little Longstone* is Headstone Head: famous view over Monsal Dale, with the Wye flowing through the valley, and the railway viaduct and cuttings of the old Midland Railway, to which Ruskin objected so strongly: "this valley is now desecrated in order that a Buxton fool may be able to find himself at Bakewell in twelve minutes." Alas, he can do so no longer: the line is closed.

Lullington (17). Small pretty village in the extreme S of the county, dominated by the broach spire of the church. This looks fourteenth century; in fact it is a careful rebuilding of 1766—an interesting event for that date. The church itself is of 1861. Monuments to Colville family (nineteenth century); many gay Victorian tiles in sanctuary.

Mackworth (14). Just outside Derby suburbia: the village street is off the main Ashbourne road, and is surprisingly secluded. The church stands by itself in a field to the E. Tall Perp. tower and spire, and much Perp. work in the body of the church. The tower (with crossbow loopholes) and S porch both have a severe defensive-looking character. Monuments to Mundy family, of Markeaton Hall (demolished since the war), and much exuberant Victorian decoration within; the lectern is a particularly remarkable nineteenth-century extravaganza. At the other end of the village is the late fifteenth-century Gatehouse—all that remains of the great house of the Mackworth family, which was destroyed in the seventeenth century; only the façade is left, like a piece of decorative stage scenery.

Mapleton (11). Close to the River Dove: the bridge leads over to Staffordshire and to Okeover Hall. The little church is an amusing eighteenth-century building, with W tower crowned by a diminutive

octagonal dome. Near the river stand the Clergymen's Widows' Almshouses, founded by Mr Okeover of Okeover in 1727: a fine brick house of the period, with hipped roof and stone dressings. The Manor House is also a good eighteenth-century brick building, the Dower House for Okeover, and Sandybrook Hall, on the A515 is late Georgian (1815).

Mapperley (12). Hillside village in narrow lanes between Ilkeston and Heanor, with collieries nearby, and the reservoir in Shipley Park. The Victorian church was pulled down, owing to the subsidence of the ground from the collieries, and has been replaced by a modern church of novel design on the cruck principle. Plain glass fills the W gable, and more plain windows command the view to the south.

In the west door is modern, imitation-Flemish, stained glass, with mining scenes.

Marston Montgomery (13). Good views to the hills of Staffordshire to the W. There is a half-timbered house, Manor Farm, in the centre of the village. The church has work from the Norman period onwards, but was heavily restored in 1877. The interior is attractive, with its chancel slightly raised, and good late-Victorian glass in E window and elsewhere. Norman font.

Marston-on-Dove (14). In the meadows by the river: farm roads connect the small village with the main road from Derby to Uttoxeter. The church has a tall Dec. spire, containing the oldest bell in the county. It was cast by John de Stafford at Leicester in 1360, and has "Hail Mary" on it. Wide, spacious interior, but scraped: the Georgian galleries and plastered interior survived until the 1920s. Good Dec. tracery in windows of S aisle: N and S aisle under same roof as nave (as at Weston-on-Trent). Eighteenth-century organ in original case, formerly at Sudbury Hall. George III Royals Arms, 1816.

Matlock (8). To the hurried traveller Matlock may appear uninteresting, even unattractive, with its commercialised amusements and souvenir-and-postcard shops. But to the

visitor who is prepared to wander and look, especially out of season, Matlock can be a little paradise.

Old Matlock is the district near the parish church, on the E side of the River Derwent—the old village. The village street climbs up to the church: here are the seventeenth-century Old Wheatsheaf and eighteenth-century rectory. The tower of the church is fifteenth century, the church itself a tactful and beautiful Victorian re-building (E window by Laurence Lee, sixteenth-century tomb to Anthony Woolley of Riber Hall). Matlock Bridge is fifteenth century, widened in the twentieth.

The warm spring was hardly known until the end of the seventeenth century: the Old Bath was made in 1698. Other springs were discovered progressively, and by the end of the nineteenth century Matlock had reached its height of fame and popularity. Over a spring at Dimple (not far from Smedley's Hydro) is a stone inscribed "1824 ALLEN HILL SPAW RESTORED".

Matlock Bank (to the N) grew up in the nineteenth century. John Smedley founded his great Hydro here in 1853. It is now the head-quarters of the Derbyshire County Council. It is an amazing building: from the back (where the main entrance is) in Smedley Street it is grim beyond belief: on each side of the street, connected by a bridge, the building rises like a vast factory. On the garden side (especially the later half of the building, 1885, by Statham, with its tower and iron corona) over-looking its terrace garden, it appears like an enormous seaside hotel. There are some imposing Victorian interiors; the domed winter garden (with grotto) is a building of charm.

Not far away is All Saints (1883, by Healey), with its beautiful Morris E window (1905). Also The Lindens —the centre block survives of the boarding house where Rossetti stayed with Elizabeth Siddall in 1857. And towering above all, it seems, is Rockside Hydro (by R. Barry Parker, 1905), now part of the College of Education, a later building of some distinction: it rises almost pagoda-like over the whole town. Just below

St John Baptist, MATLOCK Bath, by Guy Dawber, 1897

is the engine house of the old tramway, which ran down the steep hill into the centre of the town, where there is the pretty little tramway shelter, in the public gardens, surmounted by a clock.

Dale Road, the chief shopping street (notice Bank House, eighteenth century—Williams Deacons Bank), leads to Matlock Bath. First there are the Victorian houses of N Parade, then the early eighteenth-century houses, cottages and shops of S Parade. These run along the side of the river—and the valley here has become a gorge. Opposite is the domed Pavilion (1910). Behind tower the Heights of Abraham, romantic cliffside gardens, with the 1844 Victoria Tower at the top.

Matlock Bath grew up round the Old Bath (1698) and the Old Bath Hotel was established in that year. In the eighteenth century it became

known as a resort for "persons of quality"—but in Regency times it really came into its own. There is an early Victorian church with a spire of some originality (by Flockman of Sheffield, 1842), and the New Bath Hotel next door is early nineteenth century; Ruskin stayed there in 1829. The best thing to do is to walk up the road nearby which points to the Temple Hotel (originally an overflow for the Old Bath Hotel). Halfway up is an enchanting view of the houses on the hillside. There are two Gothick castellated houses—one near the top painted pink, the house for the Keeper of the Heights of Abraham, and another, painted grey, called the Lower Tower. "Waterloo Road" dates other endearing houses and cottages—Belle Vue, Belmont, a Swiss cottage, an octagonal lodge, Gilderoy House (1829): here is the full atmosphere of an early nine-

teenth-century resort. But the best thing of all is to climb up Cliff Road, to the little chapel of St John Baptist, designed by Sir Guy Dawber in 1897. This is a very special little church, built and endowed by Mrs Harris of The Rocks (the house alongside, with a terrace garden filled with statues), to be a High Church chapel-of-ease to the parish church. Inside it has all the furnishings complete of the great artist-designer: rood screen, reredos, pews and stalls, painted plasterwork of vines and roses. The road leads on to Cliff House: there are views through trees to Riber Castle opposite, and all along the dale.

Down the hill, and along the main road again, are Fountain Villas, which look Georgian, but are in fact 1850. At the Midland Hotel (note the magnificent cast-iron lamps) is the

MELBOURNE ▷

entrance to Matlock Bath Station—a gem of a station, built like a small Swiss chalet.

The personality of John Smedley still pervades the town—just as the great ruin of Riber Castle, the house which he built for himself, still dominates the skyline. (See Riber.) The hosiery mill at Lea was established by Thomas Smedley; his son John introduced modern machinery in about 1840. It was he who after successfully employing hydropathic treatment on his own workpeople established the great Hydro which made Victorian Matlock famous.

Melbourne (14). A little town in the S of the county, close to Leicestershire; famous for its church, its Hall and its associations with Australia.

The manor and rectory were originally granted to the Bishop of Carlisle on the foundation of the see in 1133, and the church is one of the most splendid Norman parish churches in England. The interior of the nave is specially grand; it is also most numinous. Tall circular piers lead the eye to the crossing. The central tower is carried on great solid piers, and above the arches, on all four sides, are arched openings—giving into nave and transepts, and originally into chancel as well. The chancel was originally apsidal, and of equal height with the nave; the present square E end is late fifteenth century. The upper part of the tower is early seventeenth century; there

MELBOURNE Hall: ▷
The Four Seasons Monument

are low Norman towers at the W end.

Melbourne Hall is to the E of the church, and the stables and older parts of the house are close to the road; through the gates to the S the road leads past a sheet of water called Melbourne Pool to the visitors' entrance. The older portions of the house represent the residence of the Bishops of Carlisle; in the early seventeenth century this was leased from the bishops by Sir John Coke, a younger son of the Coke family of Trusley, who became Principal Secretary of State to Charles I. Sir John's successors subsequently bought the

MELBOURNE Hall: The Lime Walk

property from the Bishop, and the house was enlarged and tidied up. The S front with its deep recess (as at Sutton Scarsdale) was built in 1725 by Francis Smith, and finally the garden (E) front by William Smith in 1744. This is a most decorative façade, and looks over the garden.

Sir John Coke's great grandson, Thomas Coke, was Vice-Chamberlain to Queen Anne and George I, and it was he who was responsible for laying out the garden. This was done, before the additions to the house, by the royal gardeners, London and Wise; a letter of 1696 survives, referring to two plans by Mr Wise for the garden "to suit with Versailles". The plan of the garden as executed is clever: it is not big, but by its careful planning and subdivision it seems big and full of mystery. The lawns and three wide paths with broad steps lead down to a large formal pool, across which stands Robert Bakewell's magical wrought-iron Birdcage. This, recently restored, is resplendent with gilt and colour. To the S grass walks lead off through seemingly distant vistas to fountains, or statues, or the great Four Seasons Monument, the work of Jan van Nost, and the gift of Queen Anne. There is a long yew tunnel, and a rocky grotto with wishing well:

"Rest, weary stranger in this
    shady cave,
  And taste, if languid, of the
    mineral wave."

At unexpected turns are the figures of little lead cupids, fighting, or embracing, or stringing their bows.

The whole garden is a rare survival; there is none more perfect in England.

Thomas Coke, its creator, had no son, and it was by the marriage of his second daughter that the property passed into the Lamb family. Peniston Lamb, when created a peer in 1770, took the title of Lord Melbourne. His son, the second Lord Melbourne, was Queen Victoria's first Prime Minister, and it was after him that the city of Melbourne in Australia was named. Lord Melbourne's niece married Lord Palmerston, another of Queen Victoria's Prime Ministers. It subsequently passed (through the female line) to the present owner, the twelfth Marquis of Lothian.

The house is not large. There are delightful rooms, with pictures and furnishings of the seventeenth and eighteenth centuries. It is open to the public regularly in the summer. Lord Melbourne's room is shown, and there are relics of him, of Lord Palmerston, and of Richard Baxter, seventeenth-century Nonconformist, who wrote here part of *The Saints' Everlasting Rest*.

Mickleover (14). On the outskirts of Derby; the usual shops are beginning to crowd along the main road, but there are lanes into the country behind. The church is mediaeval, but much restored in the nineteenth century. Dark interior with Victorian stained glass and plenty of pitch pine. The Mental Hospital in bright red brick is neo-Tudor of 1849.

Middleton-by-Wirksworth (00). Bluff little quarrying village; Hopton-

wood stone quarries in the parish. Pretty neo-Perp. church of 1847 by Newton, like a little chantry chapel. Interior with W gallery and finely crested cornice, beautifully furnished and recently redecorated.

Milford (11). In the Derwent valley, S of Belper. It grew up in the early nineteenth century under the aegis of Jedediah Strutt, who established a mill here in 1780. Derwent Bridge, 1790. Church of 1848, by Moffatt, partner of Scott.

The best of the old mills have been demolished; the splendid clock is preserved in the Derby Museum.

Miller's Dale and **Monsal Dale** (4/8). These two dales constitute the valley of the Wye where it diverges from the Buxton–Bakewell road, which takes a short cut over Taddington. They are well worth the detour. "There was a rocky valley between Buxton and Bakewell once upon a time", wrote Ruskin in his celebrated outburst on the coming of the railway, "divine as the Vale of Tempe; you might have seen the gods there morning and evening—Apollo and all the sweet muses of the light, walking in fair procession on the lawns of it, and to and fro among the pinnacles of its crags . . . you enterprised a railroad through the valley . . . the valley is gone and the gods with it." The railway is now closed, but the viaducts and bridges remain, mellowed by time; they enhance the

At NEW MILLS ▷

scene. There is a small hamlet near the little Victorian Gothic church of Miller's Dale, with nineteenth-century mills—the original corn mill gave the name to the dale. At *Cressbrook* is perhaps the most beautiful of all Derbyshire mills, built in 1815, with four-bay pediment, hipped roof and cupola.

Monyash (7). A bleak but beautiful spot in the High Peak; the small village was once a market town, with a three-day fair at Trinity, and a great lead-mining centre. Large village pond; the base of the old market cross survives. The church is largely Perp., but the sedilia and piscina are Transitional. Spacious building, with wide transepts. Battlemented tower and spire. Fifteenth-century font. Enormous ancient chest.

Morley (12). The church and eighteenth-century rectory (now the Diocesan Retreat House) make an attractive group, away from the main road. The church is one of the best in the county, owing to the tombs and stained glass, which give atmosphere to the interior.

The glass came from Dale Abbey at the Dissolution, and was largely the glass made for the cloisters there in 1482. There are at least three windows more or less filled with original glass, and others which have been repaired and made up with good reproduction glass of 1847; a further window (N aisle) is by Burlison and Grylls, 1875.

The church is full of interest: the nave is Norman; the tower, chancel and N chapel are late fourteenth or early fifteenth century, as we know from the very unusual brass inscriptions to the Statham family, which give details of the building process ("qui campanile istud et ecclesiam fieri fecerunt"—states the brass to Ralph Statham, who died in 1380, and his wife Goditha). The brass to John Statham, who died in 1453, records that he built the S chapel. There are other memorials to Stathams, whose heiress married John Sacheverell, who was killed on Bosworth field in 1485 (memorial in S chapel). Between the chancel and N chapel is the tomb, with inset brass, to Sir Henry Sacheverell (d. 1558), and in the N chapel itself the

recumbent effigy of their daughter Katherine, wife of Thomas Babington of Dethick. There are other Sacheverell tombs; suffice to mention the alabaster tomb to Jacynth (d. 1656) and his wife, with its inscription recording that he was a Papist ("Ille Papam humaniter Christum religiose colens Fidem Romanam orthodoxam charitatem tenens . . ."); and the baroque tomb to Robert (d. 1714), with urns and draperies. The series continues with further monuments to their heirs, the Sitwells and Wilmot Sitwells.

Near the main road is Morley Manor, a stone neo-Elizabethan house, built for the Sacheverell-Batemans in 1900 by Bodley, and now a children's home.

Morton (9). Colliery country. Church much rebuilt in mid nineteenth century. Perp. W tower. Interior of pleasant furnishings: seventeenth-century pulpit; gaily coloured chancel screen; art nouveau W screen. Lychgate designed by Gladwyn Turbutt of Ogston Hall; The Sitwell Arms across the road; eighteenth-century stone rectory with Venetian window next to the church.

Mugginton (11). A hillside village, seemingly remote, though not far from the Derby–Ashbourne road. The church has a Norman W tower, and an unrestored interior. Many box pews (and a few older ones). Fifteenth-century screen to SE chapel. Large brasses to Nicholas Kniveton and his wife (*c.* 1475). Fragments of old heraldic glass in E window of chapel—clear glass generally, and old roofs.

The Kniveton family, once of some importance, lived at *Mercaston*, where the old hall survives, now a farmhouse. Sir Andrew, the 3rd Bt, impoverished by the Civil War, sold the place in 1654.

Intake Chapel, or Halter Devil Chapel, is a mile to the NW on the road from Cross-o-th'-hands to Brailsford, and is attached to a farmhouse. The story of its origin is that Francis Brown, a farmer, one stormy night swore that he would ride into Derby "even if he had to halter the devil himself". On leading his horse from the pasture to the

stable, lantern in hand, he discovered that the horse had horns, and in a flash of lightning he thought he saw the devil, and fainted. On recovering, and repenting his past, he built this little chapel and endowed it with his property. It is a small stone-faced building of 1723.

Netherseal (17). In pleasant wooded country close to the borders of Leicestershire, Staffordshire and Warwickshire. Church much rebuilt in nineteenth century, but imposing and not lacking in atmosphere. Perp. tower. Thirteenth-century nave. Engraved stone to Roger Douton, rector (d. 1500) in chancel. Modest memorials in organ chamber to Gresleys, Rectors and Baronets (see Drakelowe). The most distinguished Gresley of Netherseal was Sir Nigel, chief mechanical engineer to L.N.E.R., and designer of the famous "Coronation" and "Silver Jubilee" Pacific locomotives. He is buried here, and was grandson of the Revd Sir Nigel (the 9th Bart), who was Rector of Seal. Eighteenth-century stone Hall, still with mullioned windows. Comfortable-looking nineteenth-century rectory.

New Mills (4). A small industrial town, redolent of the early nineteenth-century industrial development of Northern England, and taking its name from a corn mill established on the Goyt, in the old district of Ollersett. With its old factories and warehouses (some now mere shells), its old cottages, Nonconformist chapels, railway sidings and viaducts, it is of real interest to the industrial archaeologist. St George's Church was erected in 1831; it is in what Kelly calls "the pointed style". It has a W spire, and all the features of the spidery Gothic of this period—lancet windows, galleries and thin columns —a building by no means lacking in charm. St James the Less, with almshouses adjoining, was built in 1880, by W. Swinden Barber, as a memorial to James Ingham, a local philanthropist. There are mural paintings on the N wall, and stained-glass windows by Kempe. The R.C. church (1843) with spire stands prominently on the hill to the W of the town.

Bladon Castle near NEWTON SOLNEY

Newton Solney (14). The last parish in Derbyshire along the road from Repton to Burton. It is here that the Dove flows into the Trent, and there are fine views over the river. Several houses of note, especially the two white stuccoed houses (one with iron balconies and Gothick windows) on each side of the main road. Newton Park, large and early Victorian, stands back, and is now an hotel. Pretty cast-iron verandah on garden side.

The church has a short spire and its core is mediaeval, but its low, dark interior is largely Victorianised. Three thirteenth- and fourteenth-century tombs with recumbent effigies to the de Solney family. Distinguished marble monument to Sir Henry Every, 3rd Bt of Egginton, by Carter. He is semi-reclining, and dressed in Roman attire. In the churchyard is the tombstone to Thomas Gayfere (d. 1827), London mason and architect, who carried out the restoration of Westminster Hall and Henry VII's Chapel.

Half a mile to the SW on a wooded hilltop stands Bladon Castle, an early nineteenth-century brick castellated house, designed by Sir Jeffry Wyatville for Mr Hoskins of Newton Park. It was originally an eye-catcher, known as Hoskins' Folly, but was later converted into a house; it is splendid in either role.

Norbury (10). Wooded and beautiful country in the valley of the Dove, close to Staffordshire. The church is fine. Small clerestoried nave, with unusually placed low-pinnacled S tower: grand Dec. chancel. This is known to have been built by Henry Kniveton, Rector of Norbury, in the second half of the fourteenth century, and with its great traceried windows is on a different scale from the nave. There is fourteenth–fifteenth-century glass (much of it grisaille), and in the chancel are the monuments of the Fitzherberts of Norbury—the senior branch of this great Derbyshire family. Of special note are those to Nicholas (d. 1473) and Sir Ralph (d. 1483), both with alabaster effigies and much detail, such as the little figure of the monk with cowl and rosary at the feet of Sir Ralph. In the centre of the chancel is the brass to Sir Anthony (d. 1583). The family were loyal Roman Catholics throughout penal times, and suffered in consequence (see Grindleford). The celebrated Mrs Fitzherbert, wife of George IV, was a member of the family. On the death of Sir John Fitzherbert in 1649, Norbury passed to a cousin, William Fitzherbert of Swynnerton, Staffordshire, which thereupon became the chief home of the family and where they still live: Norbury subsequently decayed. It passed into other hands in the nineteenth century, and a large Victorian house was built away from the village, which has recently been pulled down. The original Hall, standing to the W of the church, represents merely a wing of the great mediaeval mansion—to which an early eighteenth-century brick front has been added. This house has recently been bought by a descendant of the Fitzherberts and has been sympathetically restored.

South Normanton (9). Coal country. "Normanton Brights" were well known. The church was much rebuilt in 1878. There is one Norman doorway, and an interesting and unusual thirteenth-century doorway in the chancel decorated with fleur-de-lis cusps. Monuments to Revel family of Carnfield Hall (and of Ogston Hall) the Elizabethan house on the S side of the main road to Alfreton. Jedediah Strutt was born at S Normanton in 1726.

Ockbrook (15). The large village is clearly visible from the new Nottingham–Derby road. Crowning the hill to the W is the delightful group of Georgian buildings which comprise the Moravian Settlement, founded here in 1750. (The Moravians, originally a German Christian sect, had early in his life a great influence on John Wesley.) The chapel, with its white-painted cupola, is the centre of the group; there is a school alongside, founded in 1799.

The parish church was largely rebuilt in the early nineteenth century, with the exception of the mediaeval broach spire. The nave is an aisleless box, with cast-iron columns, a W gallery, and a flat ceiling. Ancient screen and stalls in the chancel, brought here in 1807 by Thomas Pares, F.S.A., from Wigston Hospital, Leicester. Three monuments in chancel by Westmacott to the Pares family, who lived at Hopwell Hall: Thomas Pares (1805), "impropriate Rector of this parish, and Patron of this church"; Mary Pares (1823); and Thomas Pares

junior (1824), the antiquary. Monument in nave, with medallion portrait, to the Revd Henry Swindell (1801), a self-effacing curate (note the touching verse). There is also a Norman font, and under the tower, in a good frame, an early carved nineteenth-century Royal Arms.

Osmaston (11). A neat estate village, with many picturesque cottages against the backcloth of the park. The church is a grand affair by Stevens of 1845, more beautiful in than out. Much lavish decoration in the chancel, and many inscriptions to the Wright family.

Francis Wright, principal owner of the Butterley Iron Works, built the great neo-Tudor mansion of Osmaston Manor in 1846–9. It was subsequently purchased by the Walker family of Liverpool (of Walker Art Gallery fame), and pulled down a few years ago by Sir Ian Walker-Okeover, when he inherited and moved to Okeover, just across the Staffordshire border. The house stood in a spectacular position with a prospect of great beauty. On the terrace now stands a kind of sepulchral altar, bearing the names of Wright the builder, Stevens the architect, and Sir Ian the demolisher. All that survives is the tower, which by a fantastic arrangement contained all the chimneys. It never worked, and conventional chimneys had to be inserted in the house after all. Fine park; the little Gothick Park Lodge, facing the lake, is the house of the agent for the Osmaston and Okeover estate.

Yeldersley Hall, the pleasant Georgian house across the main Ashbourne road, was also a home of the Wright family.

Overseal (17). Much ribbon development along the main road, serving the colliery community of the district. Two good Georgian houses at S end of the village; their presence just here seems a little mysterious. At crossroads in the centre is the aisleless, barn-like church, with narrow W tower, oddly arranged inside with pews across the nave. On W wall a tablet commemorates Elizabeth Pycroft: "the land for the site of this chapel and chapelyard was the free gift of this charitable lady, in

addition to a donation towards the building, of which she laid the foundation stone, August 27, 1840." The architect was Thomas Johnson.

Padley (5). See Grindleford.

Parwich (11). Well-built stone village, prettily set in the hills NE of Ashbourne. Big Victorian–Norman church (by Robinson of Derby) built in 1873. In the tower the original Norman chancel arch and N doorway have been re-set. The latter has a carved tympanum, showing the Lamb of God with a cross, a stag trampling on a serpent, and other animals. Fine George I Royal Arms. Parwich Hall is a tall, brick house of 1747, built against the hillside, with a flight of steps up to the front door, and beautiful terrace garden.

Peak Forest (4). A bleak, straggling village in the gorgeous high country between Tideswell and Chapel-en-le-Frith. The original church, dedicated to King Charles the Martyr, was built in 1657 by Christian Bruce, wife of the 2nd Earl of Devonshire. It was extra-parochial, and independent of episcopal jurisdiction, and became famous for "Gretna Green" marriages. The practice continued until the early nineteenth century, and brought the incumbent considerable income. The new church was built in 1878, an imposing but somewhat cold Victorian building. The Venetian window and porch of the old church were re-used in the village reading room.

Pentrich (11). A village on the edge of industrialism, but intact. Wide views to Ripley and Butterley across disused railway sidings and dumps.

The church is set over the village up many steps. Pinnacled Perp. tower. Spacious light nave, with late Norman arcades. Norman font, with base dated 1662: this was rescued in the middle of the last century from the basement of a house in Ripley, where a former churchwarden had used it for salting beef. Seventeenth–eighteenth-century monuments to Horne family, former owners of Butterley Hall (see Ripley).

NORBURY ▷

102

Pinxton (12). Colliery village close to the Notts borders; streets of drab red cottages climb the hills, and the church stands a little aside on the edge of the village. Most of this is a rebuilding of 1750, set at right angles to the old church of which only the thirteenth-century tower remains; an aisle and porch were added in 1939, so that the church now presents a curious appearance. Venetian E window. Painting attributed to Guido Reni in Lady Chapel, given by the Pope to General George Manley, who commanded the Papal Guard (he had fought at Waterloo), and by General Coke of Brookhill to this church. Tablets to the Coke family. In a wooded dip in the road towards Sutton-in-Ashfield are the large gate-piers to Brookhill Hall, the home of Mr Roger Coke, the composer. Originally a Jacobean house, it was Georgianised in the late eighteenth century. China was made at Pinxton for a brief period in the eighteenth century under the aegis of the Coke family: in the Gothick library at Milton Manor in Berkshire is a Pinxton china tea set, painted with views of that house, made in 1796. (See *The Pinxton China Factory*, by C. L. Exley, published by R. Coke-Steel, Trusley, 1963.)

Pleasley (9). The road from Mans-field crosses the Notts–Derbyshire border here. Mining country, with the usual accompaniment of railway lines and sidings and abandoned stations. The church stands a short distance to the N of the main road. Perp. tower. Norman chancel arch and font.

Quarndon (11). Now a salubrious suburb of Derby. In the seventeenth century the chalybeate spring began to attract patients and visitors, and in the eighteenth the Scarsdales built the imposing inn (now Bath Farm) as a spa hotel. It was empty for some years, but has now been reopened as an hotel (1971). Dr Johnson and Admiral Rodney were among the distinguished visitors in the eighteenth century. Alas, the spring dried up in 1897! Only the little embattled Gothic well-house survives, by the side of the road near the church.

◁ The Moravian Chapel
at OCKBROOK

Victorian Gothic church of 1874 (by Giles and Brooklands).

Radburne (14) has been the home of the Chandos-Pole family since the early fifteenth century: Sir Peter de la Pole (d. 1432) married the heiress of the Chandos family, who had been at Radburne since the thirteenth century. The church is thirteenth and fourteenth century: NW Perp. tower. Bench-ends and other woodwork from Dale Abbey. Many monuments to Poles (two of them fifteenth century), and great tomb of German Pole, by Grinling Gibbons, 1684.

Radburne Hall was rebuilt, prob-ably by Francis Smith of Warwick, *c.* 1750. Handsome red-brick house on stone base, with grand flight of steps to the hall and other principal rooms on the piano nobile. Fine rococo plasterwork, and marble chimney pieces. Prince Charles Edward lunched with the family in 1745 when he reached Derby. The park is private, and the house is not open to the public.

Renishaw (6). "You see," said Sir George Sitwell to Evelyn Waugh, surveying the view from the terrace at Renishaw Hall, "you see, there is *no one* between us and the Locker-Lampsons." The Locker-Lampsons lived at Barlborough Hall, two miles away, on high ground to the E. In the valley at their feet, "half hidden in mist, lay farms, cottages, villas, the railway, the colliery and the densely teeming streets of men who worked there. They lay in shadow; the heights beyond were golden." (*Laughter in the Next Room*, p. 349.)

To readers of Sir Osbert Sitwell's autobiography, *Left Hand, Right Hand*, Renishaw will already be legendary, and the close proximity of Park and Hall to the industrial village at its feet will be no surprise. The Sitwells came to Renishaw in 1625, and the core of the house is of that date. The family established the first ironworks here in the seven-teenth century, and so re-established their fortune, nearly lost in the royal service in the Civil War. The house was enlarged at the end of the eighteenth century by Joseph Badger of Sheffield: for its fairy-tale Gothick exterior, its distinguished late-Georgian interior, and for its literary

associations it is memorable indeed. The gardens were laid out by Sir George Sitwell at the end of the last century; from the terrace it is difficult to detect any trace of the Industrial North.

The foundation stone of the un-finished village church was laid by Bishop King of Lincoln in 1902.

Repton (14). Although not far from the coalfields of Swadlincote or the breweries of Burton-on-Trent, and although oppressed by its terrible new neighbour, the Power Station of Willington, Repton maintains its ancient role. In the seventh cen-tury it was the capital of Mercia and had a flourishing monastery. The Danes swept all away in 875, but in the tenth century, a new church was built—and of this building the crypt survives. In 1172 an Augustin-ian priory was founded here from Calke, and a great cruciform church was built to the east of the parish church. Of this some of the founda-tions survive, together with the priory arch and the west wing of the cloister court—all now part of Repton School.

The crypt of the parish church is one of the most complete Saxon buildings left in England. The short chancel above it is also part of this ancient church, though the lancet windows are thirteenth-century inser-tions. A nave of six bays was added in the fourteenth century, together with the tower and spire, 212 feet high.

At the dissolution the Priory buildings were sold to Thomas Thacker, whose son Gilbert pulled nearly everything down (saying that he would destroy the nest for fear that the birds should build there again). An alabaster slab (1563) to his memory is in the south aisle of the church. There are later Thacker monuments, and a Royal Arms of George III.

Sir John Port of Etwall left money to found a school at Etwall or Repton, and his executors bought the remain-ing wing of the Priory to house this school. Under the headmastership of Dr Pears (1854–74) the school grew enormously, like other old founda-tions in the Victorian era. The Pears Memorial Hall was built in his memory by Sir Arthur Blomfield

RENISHAW ironworks

(1883–6). This stands on part of the site of the priory church, and its foundations are clearly visible. Stevens had built the school chapel in 1857: in 1957, to celebrate the quatercentenary, the new theatre was built by Marshall Sisson. The Hall, the headmaster's house, with its seventeenth-century front, is to the N of the priory. It incorporates part of Prior Overton's tower, which had been built in the mid-fifteenth century overlooking the Trent meadows. The priory, with its Norman crypt, houses the school library and museum.

The school dominates the pleasant little town. School boarding-houses are easily recognisable (New House, 1909, is by W. A. Forsyth). There are one or two good buildings in the town, such as the late Georgian house called The Croft, opposite the Town Cross; one or two small timber-framed houses; The Grange (early eighteenth-century) at the S end of the town; and Easton House, built in 1907 for a housemaster by Sir Edwin Lutyens.

Pretty country to the S: Repton Park, with its lake and waterfall and ancient trees, contained until the late nineteenth century a square castellated toy-fort house belonging to the Harpur-Crewes; fragmentary relics of the stables of this long-forgotten house are hidden in the woods. Nearby is another Gothick house of much the same date, called The

Hayes—gay and gabled with great battlemented porch.

Riber (8). The great towers and battlements of John Smedley's Castle look down from their height above Matlock—but Riber can only really be approached by a circuitous route via Tansley or Cromford. Smedley, the great hosiery manufacturer and founder of the Matlock Hydro, built the castle to his own design in 1862. After the death of his widow it became a boys' prep school, and so continued till 1929. It numbers Sir John Summerson, the architectural historian, curator of Sir John Soane's Museum, among its old boys. After standing empty for ten years, it was used as a government food store during the war—since when it has decayed and is now a roofless shell. The grounds are now utilised as a Fauna Reserve, which is open to the public.

To the E of the castle, close to the road, are two good seventeenth-century stone houses, Riber Hall and Riber Manor House, with gables, mullioned windows, and stone gate-piers—buildings of great charm.

Riddings (12). In the colliery area close to the Notts border. There is a good Gothick church of 1832, of the Commissioners' type: wide aisleless nave, lancet windows, spire and pinnacles. It has all been recently redecorated.

Ripley (12). The industrial town grew out of the ironworks at Butterley in the early nineteenth century. Benjamin Outram, the engineer, of Butterley Hall—founder with Thomas Jessop and Francis Wright of the Butterley Works—introduced railways into collieries, and it was here that the iron roof of St Pancras Station was made in 1868. It was the second syllable of his name that gave us the word "tram". His son, Sir James Outram, became famous as soldier and administrator in India.

Ripley Church was built in 1820, through the energy of the Vicar of Pentrich, after the Pentrich "rebellion" of 1817, when disgruntled workers of the neighbourhood staged an insurrection. It is of the Commissioners' type, with very wide, aisleless interior and SW tower.

There is a large Market Square, with characteristic tall nineteenth-century Town Hall in flaming red brick. Butterley Hall afterwards became the offices of the Butterley Company, and there are modern blocks of offices in the yet rural park. It is now the County Police Headquarters.

Risley (15). Still just succeeds in disentangling itself from the suburban growth of Sandiacre—but is nearly murdered by roads: the new by-pass

RENISHAW Hall ▷

roars past on its embankment a short distance to the S, and the old main road cuts right through the village like a great runway. This is not the way to set off an interesting group of village buildings—which Risley indeed possesses. First, there is the little church, built by Michael Willoughby in 1593 as the private chapel of the Hall—an example of very late Gothic. Contemporary font decorated with the Willoughby Arms. Endearing little dolls' house tower. The Willoughbys' house has gone: a late Georgian brick house occupies the site, with a long stable building of Elizabethan date at right angles. The terrace by the moat survives, with old balustrading—and beautifully planted with trees. Opposite, and standing at the E end of the church, is perhaps the most perfect early-eighteenth-century house in Derbyshire. It is dated 1706. Very distinguished little façade, with the Willoughby Arms on an escutcheon above the door, stone quoins, hipped roof, keystones carved with female faces, sash windows, mellow red brick. But it is empty and crumbling, and cries out for a rescuer. Further

to the E is the little group of the Willoughby schools, built in 1718: two handsome tall schoolrooms, with long windows with their leaded lights and wooden mullions and transomes —and the master's house (with shell-hood door) set slightly back between them. (See Wilne.)

Rosliston (17). A rural village, despite the proximity of Drakelowe and Swadlincote. Endearing little church of 1819, built on to a diminutive fourteenth-century tower and spire with heavily buttressed base. Thomas Stretton, "an able and experienced workman", was the builder of the new church, and it cost £702 11s. 0d. The light shines attractively through clear Gothic windows. Heraldic fragment of seventeenth-century monument on S wall.

Rowsley (8). Rowsley grew in importance with the advent of the Midland Railway, but the famous line to Manchester is now closed. The original station (by Sir Joseph Paxton, 1849) still stands, but where the line and all its sidings were is now a wasteland. The River Wye remains

beautiful, and Rowsley bridge dates from the seventeenth century. The Peacock is an attractive hostelry, resort of fishermen; the house itself was built in 1652 by John Stevenson, agent to the Manners family at Haddon, as the inscription over the front door tells us. The church is 1855 Norman by Salvin, and contains the marble tomb and effigy of Lady John Manners, by Calder Marshall (1859). Ninth-century Anglo-Saxon cross-head, recovered from the river-bed.

Sandiacre (15). The new Nottingham–Derby main road (A52) here drives high over railway lines, sidings, factories, houses, and the River Erewash, and soon crosses the M1; at the river is the frontier. Half a mile to the N, across all this conglomeration, on high, sandy ground, stands Sandiacre Church, with its plain but lofty Norman nave, still loftier Dec. chancel, and W tower with broach spire. It is not at first easy to find, as the streets through the town conceal the view of the church, and the road up the rocky little hill on which it stands seems to peter out

RIBER Castle from behind

beyond it. But it repays the search. On entering, the tall aisleless nave seems dark by comparison with the lofty chancel, ablaze with light and colour beyond the Norman arch. This chancel was built by Roger de Norbury, Bishop of Lichfield, who held the Prebend of Sandiacre from 1342–7. Great traceried windows, elaborate canopied sedilia and piscina, exterior resplendent with pinnacled buttresses and quatrefoil parapet.

Sawley (15). The urban growth of Long Eaton stretches mercilessly along the main road, but there are old houses, and some village atmosphere, round the church. Beyond is the Trent, with its busy marina for small boats. The church is of special interest. Exceptionally wide nave. Norman chancel arch. Perp. chancel screen. Old timber roof. Seventeenth-century pulpit. Ancient chancel stalls. Stone screen behind high altar. Mediaeval monuments and brasses to the Boothe family, who supposedly built the fifteenth-century tower and spire. But the greatest feature of interest is the late Perp. projecting bay on the S side of the chancel, with panelled sides and vaulted roof, containing the tomb of John Boothe, Treasurer of Lichfield Cathedral (1496).

In the flat country to the east the

five lines of the Midland Railway to London, Burton, Derby, Chesterfield and Nottingham join, and form remarkable contortions of rail on the map. But the celebrated Trent station is no more.

Scarcliffe (9). The mining village of Shirebrook is not far away, but this is a rural place, dominated by the tower of the church, rebuilt in 1842. The church itself is ancient, but the interior is scraped and snail-pointed. Transitional arcade with early English capitals. Norman door. Odd, long Tudor windows in nave. Colourful Victorian east window. Pretty seventeenth-century font cover. Enormous mediaeval chest. Unusual large effigy in nave of a lady and her child, said to be Constantia de Frecheville, c. 1175. This is beautiful and original: the child holds a scroll with inscription (hard to decipher) and the figures are supported on a grinning lion. Beautiful lettering on ledger stone in NE chapel (note the names of the daughters).

Scropton (14). The railway line to Derby and Burton from Uttoxeter runs here alongside the River Dove; there are views up to Tutbury Castle on the hill to the S—but this is across the border in Staffordshire. 1856 church by Benjamin Ferrey, with pyramid roof to the tower, and

an early sixteenth-century tomb within to Nicholas Agard and his two wives—one a Vernon, the other a Ferrers.

Shardlow (15). The first village in Derbyshire for the traveller on the A6; and, with its many old commercial buildings on the banks of the Trent and the canal, a very good sight indeed. There are wharves and warehouses, a brewery and ropewalk, a workhouse—the "House of Industry", built in 1821—and canal locks and bridges.

Originally there was a ferry over the river, called the Wilden Ferry. The Cavendish Bridge was built in 1771, and demolished by the floods of 1947. The new bridge was built in 1956; at the approach to the bridge a plaque lists the old tolls originally levied on the first bridge. The Trent and Mersey Canal was built between 1766 and 1777 to serve the needs of the Potteries and the Midlands; it joined the Bridgewater Canal near Runcorn, and James Brindley was the engineer. It is still open.

The severe stone façade of Shardlow Hall looks well from the road. The E side is dated 1684; the W side, facing the garden, is of brick, and dated 1726. The house was built by Leonard Fosbrooke, the magnate of the Shardlow Port: the Sutton family took over the port and succeeded to

the house, which is used as offices by the Ministry of Agriculture. There are several other fine houses, notably the stone house nearest the bridge, called Broughton House, the offices of Messrs Stevens. The church is a good building of 1838 in the Perp. style: embattled tower, with aisleless nave and W gallery, and cast-iron traceried windows.

Shirebrook (9) finds no place in most guidebooks to Derbyshire: it is a small colliery town on the Notts border, dominated by Shirebrook and Langwith collieries. There are grim streets of miners' houses, enlivened by the occasional bizarre flash of such buildings as the Railway Hotel or the Empire Cinema (Bingo Hall); and a big shabby Market Square. The church has a Victorian Norman S aisle—the original church —to which a spacious Gothic nave has been added later. The chancel has never been built. Instead, a high altar with high dorsal stands at the blocked east end, with great hanging crucifix and fine ornaments—an effective treatment. Wheel window above with modern figure of Christ between the arms of the two ducal families of Cavendish, Devonshire and Portland.

Shirley (11). The family of Shirley of Staunton Harold take their name from this place and own land here. The small church was largely rebuilt in the nineteenth century; the interior is crammed with highly varnished pews, and there is a W gallery on iron columns. Beautiful countryside near Ashbourne.

Shirland (9). Traffic roars past on the A61 from Alfreton to Chesterfield: this is industrial Derbyshire— but beautiful country is near. Embattled Perp. church with clerestories and pinnacled tower. Well-furnished interior, with early Italian painting in altar frame, and many monuments. The earliest (in chancel) is fourteenth century and bears the arms of Grey de Shirland. Sixteenth-century tomb-chest (N aisle) to John Revell of Ogston (d. 1537). Eighteenth-century tablet, richly decorated with fruit and flowers, to John Revell, 1708.

Ogston Hall, a mile to the W, overlooks the valley of the Amber and up to the high ground on which the village stands. To the north is the newly-formed reservoir. The Revells built the mediaeval house here, of which a good deal survives, though added to in the seventeenth century, again in the eighteenth, and yet again in the nineteenth. The Turbutts, who married the Revell heiress, built a handsome new E front in 1768 (architect, E. Stanley of Chesterfield), slightly altered by William Lindley of Doncaster a decade or two later. This was all Victorianised and mediaevalised by Hine of Nottingham (1864 onwards) who also added the tower and the gables on the S front. It is a romantic and fascinating house, still the home of the Turbutt family. There are dramatic views through the gatehouse to the reservoir to the N, which has made Ogston like a lakeside fairy castle.

To the S of Shirland village, clearly visible from the main road to Alfreton, stands a small early seventeenth-century brick house with central porch, called Shirland Park. It is now a farm, but was originally a hunting lodge.

Smalley (12). On the edge of the coal country; coal has certainly been worked here since the twelfth century. Small Victorian church, formerly a chapel of Morley, with low bell tower of 1913. Stainsby House, a large plain late-eighteenth-century stone house, was built by the Wilmot-Sitwell family, successors of the Sacheverells (see Morley).

Smisby (17). Romantic position overlooking Ashby-de-la-Zouch: the Tournament Field recalls Ivanhoe. Small mediaeval church, with W tower, and containing monuments to Joan Comyn (fourteenth century) and Kendall family, who lived in sixteenth-century Hall next door, now handsome farmhouse.

Snelston (10). A shady, secluded, well-wooded valley, close to the River Dove, S of Ashbourne. Many cottages ornée; the Stanton Arms with a gay heraldic inn sign. The church stands well, on the edge of the park, looking up the hill to the fortress walls and miniature tower—all that survive—of Cottingham's Shelston Hall (1827), demolished since the war. The present squire has made a delightful home in the stables, of which the central block was part of the original late-seventeenth- or early-eighteenth-century house. This now incorporates a number of splendid Cottingham features from the demolished mansion. Gardens with lake and grand trees.

Early nineteenth-century Gothic church, with Perp. NW tower. Attractive, well-furnished interior, bright and colourful with good late nineteenth-century glass and Tractarian fittings.

Somercotes (12). Industrial growth on the edge of Notts. Attractive church (1902) by P. H. Currey.

Somersal Herbert (13). Romantic hamlet, taking its name from the great FitzHerbert family of Norbury and Tissington (q.v.), who first held the manor in the thirteenth century and are still associated with it. The Hall is an Elizabethan half-timbered manor house, built by John Fitz-Herbert and Ellen his wife, whose names and the date 1564 are recorded on a wooden tablet inside the entrance. The sight of the entrance front, with its asymmetrical arrangement of gables of different heights, and timber motifs and windows of different sizes, framed by eighteenth-century gate-piers capped with urns,

is one of great charm. Next door stands the church, somewhat rebuilt in 1874 (by C. J. Neale of Mansfield), containing a Norman font, and a monument to John FitzHerbert and his wife Mary, 1601.

Spinkhill (6). From the road from Barlborough to Renishaw the view across the valley to the N is dominated by a blackened Victorian spire: St Mary's R.C. Church, which adjoins Mount St Mary's College. An older house was converted into the rather grim but impressive buildings of the school in 1842. The church was built in 1845 (probably by A. Hansom), and has all the magnificence of a large Victorian R.C. church. The school buildings were further enlarged later in the nineteenth century, and there is a domed school chapel also, by Adrian Gilbert Scott (1930).

Spondon (15). Pronounced "Spoon-don". Great suburban sprawl, where the new Nottingham–Derby main road disgorges: a few old houses and the church stand above the dual-carriageway, surrounded by new villas. There is one good-looking three-storeyed Georgian house; the view to the S surveys a prospect of Spondon Power Station, the tower of Elvaston church, and at least three other power stations along the line of the Trent. Mediaeval church (rebuilt 1340 after a fire), much restored in nineteenth century. Stone gospel-lectern in sanctuary (cp. Taddington).

Stanley (12). Small rural village, though not far from Ilkeston or Derby. The pretty little church is somewhat Victorianised, but contains a rare Royal Arms of William III, and an entertaining painted board of 1765 in the chancel, to mark the singers' seats.

Stanton-by-Bridge (14). The Bridge is Swarkeston Bridge. The village is on the S bank of the Trent. Big, brick Georgian rectory. The little church with its bellcote has Saxon long-and-short work, Norman S doorway, and chancel arch. Interesting incised alabaster slab in chancel to William Sacheverell (1558).

Stanton-by-Dale (15). A pleasant stone village in the midst of industry.

Brick almshouses (1711) line the approach to the church, a fourteenth-century building, with Norman tympanum to S door, and Perp. tower. It is a rude surprise to walk round to the N side and look down upon the valley occupied by the vast factories and chimneys of the Stanton and Staveley Ironworks.

Stanton-in-the-Peak (8). Steep village street. One imposing three-storeyed early-eighteenth-century house, and a public house called Flying Childers. The little church with its spire was originally built (1839) as the private chapel of the Hall by the Thornhill family, but became the parish church later in the century. Of rare interest is the bronze Italian holy-water stoup of 1596; several very attractive monuments to the Thornhills, too. The Hall is well concealed in its park (it is not open to the public): the main entrance front is of 1799, and by Lindley (of Doncaster). Behind, there is a long range dated 1693, terminating in a single Jacobean gable. The Thornhills built the tower on Stanton Moor in 1832, to commemorate Earl Grey and the Reform Bill.

Stanton Moor is remarkable for its mysterious stones and barrows: in the area bounded by Alport, Stanton and Birchover are the Circle known as the Nine Ladies, the Andle Stone and the King's Stone, and the caves in Rowtor Rocks and Cratcliffe Rocks.

Staveley (6). The ancient church and seventeenth-century hall are submerged in nineteenth-century industrialism. The Stanton and Staveley Ironworks, with railway sidings and modern housing estates, dominate the scene. An octagonal lodge (with Cavendish snake over the door: was it designed by Paxton?) stands at the W end of the church. To the N stands Staveley Hall, the former home of the Frecheville family. This was built in 1604, but has in turn been Georgianised and again Jacobeanised in the nineteenth century. For long it served as the rectory, but is now council offices.

Large church, originally thirteenth century. Upper part of tower and S arcade Perp. Spacious N aisle by

Gilbert Scott, 1869. Beautiful High Church furnishings and rood screen. Triptych in St Michael's Chapel after Rubens, and splendid altar ornaments by Frank Knight of Wellingborough. Many monuments to Frechevilles: one brass in chancel includes symbol of Trinity, and another figure of B.V.M., which surprisingly survived Reformation. Notable heraldic glass in Frecheville Chapel by Henry Gyles of York, 1676. Monument in chapel to Christian Frecheville, Lady St John of Bazinge, "daughter of John Frecheville Esq., who in memory of his dearest child caused these stones to be layed together". She was the daughter of the last Frecheville, later Lord Frecheville of Staveley. "She dyed in childbed. Her infant John Pawlet surviving his mother seven dayes lyes here interred with her." Also monument, 1682, surmounted by coronet and cherubs, to Lord Frecheville himself: "Anne Charlotte, Lady Frecheville, in memory of her dearest Lord and Husband caused this monument to be erected." The date over the S door of the Frecheville chapel is 1696.

The E window of St Michael's Chapel is by Christopher Webb, and includes portions of old glass once in the rectory.

At *Barrow Hill* to the NW is an attractive late nineteenth-century church in red brick by Sir Raymond Unwin. And at *Hollingwood* to the SW is St Francis', of the mid-1930s, converted from former barn and other farm buildings.

Steetley (6). Away in the fields not far from Worksop and the heavy traffic of the A619 stands Steetley Chapel, one of the richest examples of Norman architecture in the country. For company it has a large farm, but there is no village, and its presence here in its miniature magnificence is a mystery. For two centuries it was desecrated and used as a cowshed, until restored by Pearson in 1880. It comprises a small oblong aisleless nave, a square chancel, and vaulted apse. Splendid display of carving and elaborate ornamentation on capitals and vault.

Stoney Middleton (5). Close to the entrance to Middleton Dale: to the

N the walk through the Dale leads to the celebrated pinnacle called Lover's Leap. Village of narrow, hilly streets of old houses. Stone quarries. In the eighteenth century there lived here a stone mason called Booth, who subscribed to James Paine's architectural publications. He may have designed the interesting octagonal church, built here in 1759 (or could Paine have had a hand in it himself?). It has a central lantern with lunette windows. The low Perp. W tower survives from the earlier church. The interior is disappointing —spoiled by Victorian fittings and roof. Lord Denman, Lord Chief Justice in 1832, who defended Queen Caroline at her trial, lived at the Hall, to the E of the church. It is seventeenth century, enlarged and remodelled in the nineteenth.

Sudbury (13). Sudbury is one of the best villages in Derbyshire: one long street of pretty brick cottages, and the Vernon Arms, a distinguished building of 1671, at the end. But the great experience for the traveller, whether coming from Derby or from Uttoxeter along the A516, is the first sight of Sudbury Hall, standing back a little way from the road, unprotected from the public gaze.

The house was begun in 1613 by Mary Vernon, and completed by her son George between 1670 and 1695. It is built of warm red brick, and although its owes some allegiance to Jacobean design, it is very much a house of the later seventeenth century. There is a grand frontispiece by Sir William Wilson, which has a definite Baroque quality: the hipped roof and cupola surmounted by a golden ball link it to such houses as Belton and Coleshill. The interior contains contemporary rooms of great distinction, with plasterwork by Bradby and Pettifer, ceilings painted by Laguerre, carvings by Pierce and Gibbons. There is a carved staircase of great magnificence, and a Long Gallery upstairs, filling the whole S. front.

On the death of the 9th Lord Vernon the house was transferred to the National Trust; it has been restored and redecorated under the supervision of Mr John Fowler, and is open to the public. The present Lord Vernon has built a smaller

house for himself, designed by Sir Martin Beckett, near the walled garden, and facing the lake.

The church stands next door, and is a much-restored fourteenth-century building. Many Vernon monuments, and Victorian stained glass by Burlison and Grylls.

Opposite the Hall to the N is an early-nineteenth-century eye-catcher, in the form of an embattled gatehouse.

Sutton-on-the-Hill (14). The Victorian spire is a landmark: the village clusters below. Most of the church is a rebuilding of 1841, though the nave arcade and tower itself are fourteenth century. In the chancel is a large monument of Jacobean type to Judith, wife of Samuel Sleigh (d. 1634). A black coffin takes the place of the effigy, and there is a long inscription in Latin describing her many virtues. The Sleigh family purchased the manor in 1603, and it has descended through the Cottons and Wards to the Buckstons of Bradbourne (q.v.). The Hall is a castellated Gothick house, with big traceried sash windows and two canted bays overlooking a wide soft lawn to the S. Impressive entrance court behind, with romantic machicolated turrets—all in brick and plaster, homely and lovable. Inside, several Strawberry Hill features, including a gorgeous vaulted dining room.

Sutton Scarsdale (9). From one thrilling stretch of the M1 it is possible to see, on one side of the road, the towers of Hardwick and the fairy-tale keep and long, glistening terrace of Bolsover, and, on the other, the ruins of Sutton Scarsdale.

The house here was built for Nicholas Leeke, 2nd Earl of Scarsdale, by Francis Smith of Warwick in 1724: it is now a disintegrating but grandly beautiful ruin. The baroque E front is crowned by a pediment containing the arms of the Leekes, Earls of Scarsdale; the long N front, only slightly less grand, contained the main entrance, the S front is almost built into the N side of the church, and with its rows of gaping windows dominates the poor little

The Long Gallery, ▷
SUDBURY Hall

church. Vegetation is rampant, but traces of decayed plasterwork are visible. In the early nineteenth century, (on the extinction of the Leekes) the property was bought by the Arkwrights (cp. Arkwright Town a little to the N), who abandoned the place after the Great War, on the closer approach of collieries and industry. Its new owners sold off some of the splendid interior to the U.S.A. (now in Philadelphia Museum), and the shell decayed under the threats of the demolition contractor. It was finally saved by Sir Osbert Sitwell, who bought it after the second world war in order to preserve the ruin.

The church is mediaeval: the odd thing is the entire absence of monuments to the Leekes. It seems that they were commemorated in sixteenth- and seventeenth-century glass, nearly all of which has gone. Cox (in his *Churches of Derbyshire*) quotes sources describing numerous heraldic windows existing in the eighteenth century—Leeke impaling Foljambe, Savage, Waterton, and so on. The most interesting thing in the church now is the monument to Francis Pierrepont (1707) of Oldcotes (Owlcotes). Owlcotes, in this parish, was one of the great houses built by Bess of Hardwick, and it was inherited by her daughter, Frances, who married Sir Henry Pierrepont. Francis was the last of this branch of the family. Owlcotes was pulled down after his death. There is merely a farmhouse on the site.

Swadlincote (17). "Swadlincote", writes Mr René Cutforth in his reminiscences (*Order to View*, Faber & Faber, 1969), "is a little town in S Derbyshire. It is known locally as Swad, and it is a bit of a joke, being no beauty-spot by anybody's standards. . . . I was born within a mile of Swad and lived there until I was seventeen. . . . It was so ugly it made you laugh. The whole district was a loose assemblage of gigantic holes in the ground, some of them half a mile across, where clay was dug out for the various works which made drainpipes and teapots and crockery and jugs, bowls and chamberpots, and large, hideous

vases of poisonous green to put aspidistras in. Along the edges of these great holes, dividing them one from another like threads in a spider's web, ran the dark grey spoil heaps, a tangle of derelict railway lines, and the little black streets of houses, steeply up or down hill. No proper grass grew anywhere, but a sage green vegetation like little prehistoric Christmas trees covered the older tip heaps, and at some point on every skyline the twin wheels and black scaffolding of pit-head gear would mark the shaft of a coalmine. Deep down below the clay holes the whole earth was worm-eaten with tunnels, many of them lost and forgotten for decades, so that streets were always falling in a foot or two, and most of the houses were cracked somewhere or held together with iron braces, and a sad smell of gas from broken mains hung over it all. . . ."

Swadlincote is just like that. It is the centre of the S Derbyshire coalfield, and has engulfed all the neighbourhood — Church Gresley, Newhall, Woodville: the names survive, but it is one amorphous sprawl. Many drab streets, many Nonconformist chapels, many public houses, and a Town Hall of 1861. The unexciting, aisleless, apsed church is by Stevens, of 1848.

Swanwick (12). Ignored by guidebooks, but well known for its Conference Centre, which occupies The Hayes, a comfortable Victorian house, one of the many Derbyshire houses of the Wrights of the Butterley Company. Large, prosperous Victorian church (NW tower of 1902) at the traffic lights on the main A61. Industrial countryside.

Swarkeston (14). A romantic spot close to the River Trent and the Swarkeston Bridge. Here was the great house of the Harpurs, before they moved to Calke after the Civil War. There is a small gabled house close to the river, perhaps an appendage of the great house, perhaps built to replace it. The massive walls surrounding the farm, and some of its outbuildings, contain the empty fireplaces and windows of this once great mansion.

One building that has survived,

albeit in a semi-ruinous state, is the Stand, built at the head of a rectangular walled field, which was presumably some kind of bullbaiting or gaming field. The little building consists of two small towers, crowned with little ogee domes, and between them a lower, battlemented centre, comprising a large room above, an arcaded loggia below. It was built about 1630, and Mr Mark Girouard, on grounds of stylistic affinity to Bolsover, attributes it to John Smythson. At the corner of the lane to the church is a gateway with two stout piers, surmounted by great bulbous balls.

The church was largely rebuilt in 1876. The Harpur chapel contains a number of monuments, notably the two alabaster tombs to Richard Harpur and his wife (1577) and Sir John and his wife (1627). Tomb with incised portrait to John Rolleston (1482) in the sanctuary.

Swarkeston Bridge is nearly three-quarters of a mile long, and dates from the thirteenth and fourteenth centuries. There are 17 arches and stretches of causeway across the flat meadows. The Royalists attempted to hold the bridge in 1643, but they were defeated by Sir John Gell. The Young Pretender's army reached this point in 1745, and here turned back.

Taddington (7). In the grand limestone country of Peakland: the village is now mercifully by-passed by the A6. Handsome church with spire; interior scraped but elegant. Four-bay nave arcade, lofty chancel with big flat-headed windows, stone gospel-lectern on N side of sanctuary, High Church furnishings and statues. In the S chapel is a brass (1505) to Richard Blackwall, and in the churchyard the shaft of a cross, probably of the eleventh century.

Tansley (8). In a valley to the E of Matlock. Old bleachworks, and other old industries. One or two good Georgian village houses. Little Gothic dolls-house church of 1840.

Taxal (4). Dead-end village in a lovely position overlooking the Goyt

◁ Taddington

valley S of Whaley Bridge. Wide, aiseless church of 1825, attached to Perp. W tower. Memorials to many Jodrells, beginning with William Jaudrell "the Archer" who died in 1375, and Roger Jaudrell who fought at Agincourt. Also a monument to Michael Heathcote, "Gentleman of the Pantry and Yeoman of the Mouth to his late Majesty King George II who died in 1765". Queen Anne Royal Arms. Eighteenth-century altar rails. In the village, seventeenth-century Inn called The Bells of Taxal, and on the high road to Macclesfield is the Cat and Fiddle, reputed the highest inhabited public house in England. To the E stands Shallcross Hall, an early eighteenth-century house, which belonged to the Jodrells till 1925.

Thorpe (10). On the road to Dovedale; the village lies on the slopes that lead up to the hill of Thorpe Cloud. The little church has a squat Norman tower. Norman and later work in the nave. Nineteenth-century chancel. Elizabethan altar rails, and tomb in sanctuary of John Milward (1632). Near the village is the Peveril of the Peak Hotel, recently greatly enlarged and remodelled by Trust Houses. Just across the frontier in Staffordshire is the Izaak Walton Hotel, in a superb position and with good views of Dovedale.

Tibshelf (9). Mining country; characteristic village. Most of the church is by Bodley and Garner of 1887—but not one of their grand churches. It replaces a building of 1729, and the Perp. W tower survives from the mediaeval church. Quiet, good-mannered interior. Small, late seventeenth-century brass in chancel to John Twentiman, Vicar of Tibshelf (d. 1683).

Newton Old Hall, a mile to the S, has fine gate-piers and seventeenth-century stone façade.

Ticknall (14). Grandly wooded, undulating country S of the Trent. The village has kept its character and its charm: cottages of stone and brick, backed by the noble planting in Calke Park, hedges and garden walls, the Harpur Almshouses (1772), a late Georgian Methodist Chapel

(1827)—there is nothing to spoil it, except the villas in the former vicarage garden. Broad green swards line the approach to the gates and lodges to Calke Abbey; a private railway used to cross the road by the stone arch nearby. The church is by Stevens, and one of his best: a quiet, scholarly essay in the Gothic Revival (1842). There are fragments of the mediaeval church in the churchyard. Two grand little pairs of estate cottages opposite the approach to the church; at the far end of the village the Priory is a tall, comfortable, Georgian house.

Tideswell (4). A little town lying in a secluded hollow, and surrounded by the great rolling country of the Peak. Without having any houses of special merit, the *tout ensemble* is attractive, and it is dominated by one of the finest churches in the county.

Its special interest is that it was all built at one period—during the fourteenth century. Spacious nave of five bays with lofty aisles; great transepts with enormous traceried Dec. windows; long chancel of equal height with the nave, with four big flat-headed windows in N and S walls, almost Perp. in style, and great E window of Dec. character. Externally the church is embattled and pinnacled; there is a central bellcote at the crossing, and at the W end stands the grand early Perp. tower, crowned with enormous pinnacles.

The interior is full of interest: a stone screen behind the high altar, with tall niches and canopies for figures of saints—providing a sacristy behind; Perp. font; some old choir seats and pews; original timber roof; Victorian stained glass of considerable quality—E window a Tree of Jesse, by C. G. S. Foljambe; W window by Hardman and Powell—and a number of mediaeval monuments. Of special note are the brass to John Foljambe (1383) in the chancel, and another to Sir Robert Lytton (1483); equally interesting is the brass to Bishop Pursglove, showing him dressed in pre-Reformation mass vestments, although the date is 1579. There are other monuments to Lyttons of Litton, ancestors of the Lyttons of Knebworth. The W screen is by Oldrid Scott.

The hamlet of *Litton* is to the SE of Tideswell: here there are a number of good eighteenth-century cottages and houses facing a small green with village cross, of which the steps are ancient. Many dilapidated early industrial buildings and mill wheels in the local dales: the mills in Litton Dale still flourish. *Cressbrook Mill:* see Miller's Dale.

Tissington (11). Large gate-piers and a lodge on the Ashbourne–Buxton road lead into an avenue of old lime trees—a new avenue is now being planted alongside—on and down into the village, which is all set as it were in the middle of a park. Stone cottages and houses adorn this beautifully landscaped scene; above the lane on one side stands the church, and facing the church on the other is Tissington Hall, the home of the FitzHerberts.

The church is Norman, and had a Victorian Norman arcade and aisle added in 1854. Comfortable eighteenth-century furnishings, box pews, two-decker pulpit. Early seventeenth-century standing monument to Francis (d. 1619) and Sir John Fitz-Herbert (d. 1643) with their wives, beside the chancel arch. Many family monuments in chancel of seventeenth, eighteenth and nineteenth centuries (especially one to Martha FitzHerbert, d. 1699, by Francis Bird). Royal Arms of George II.

The Hall is an early Jacobean house: the main E front is of two storeys with central porch, with eighteenth-century stables alongside to the S, and a long, lower wing wandering off to the N. This E front is enclosed in a walled garden, pierced by a handsome gateway. The W front was remodelled in the eighteenth century, and the hall contains a delicious Gothick chimneypiece *à la* Batty Langley—in addition to much good seventeenth-century panelling, both there and elsewhere in the house. The FitzHerberts of Tissington and Somersal Herbert descend from a younger son of Sir William Fitzherbert of Norbury, and first came to Tissington in the middle of the fifteenth century.

Tissington is also well known for well-dressing. There are five wells, and on Ascension Day all are dressed with flowers, berries and

mosses forming decorative pictures. The tradition is that, many centuries ago, in a time of severe drought the wells of Tissington alone did not fail. They have never failed, and the festival has always been maintained, with religious services and local festivity.

Trusley (14). The little brick church was built in 1713: baroque S door, and small W tower, interior complete with box pews and three-decker, many monuments to the Cokes, and wonderful collection of hatchments. It is recorded in the church register for 1713 that "the aforesd sixth of August was the opening of the new church, when we had both vocal and instrumental musick, the service read as at cathedrals, an anthem very well performed, Mr Coke being one of the performers". Engraved glass

screen in memory of Ronald Coke-Steel (1963) by David Peace.

The original great house of the Cokes (who first came to Trusley in 1418) stood to the W of the present Old Hall, and was pulled down in the seventeenth century. In 1902 a great new house, called the Manor, was built by General Coke further to the S. This has recently been curtailed in size and converted into flats by the family, who have now made their home in the part-Elizabethan, part-eighteenth-century Old Hall which adjoins the Stable Court near the church. The original coach house has been converted into a village hall and lined with seventeenth-century panelling from Kirkby Hall, another former Coke house in Notts. Gardens with grass walks converging on a tall Elizabethan gazebo or summer house.

Turnditch (11). On the main road between Ashbourne and Belper. Pretty little long low chapel; old SW door, date 1630 on SE door. The building was enlarged in 1882—a picture inside shows its eighteenth-century appearance, with Venetian window. List of subscribers to the rebuilding. Opposite stands the school, an endearing building with little bellcote, dated 1849.

Twyford (14). A tiny village attractively set on the banks of the Trent. Small aisleless church; a Georgian brick nave leads to a fourteenth-century chancel through a Norman chancel arch. Oil lamps in nave, tastefully used for electric light; candelabra in chancel. Large slate slab against N chancel wall commemorates Richard Harpur (1658), and his wife, daughter of Sir Edward

119

Vernon of Sudbury. An early eighteenth-century monument with illegible inscription, crowned with Harpur Arms, in the sanctuary, and late eighteenth-century monument opposite to Bristowe family. Thirteenth–fourteenth-century tower and spire.

Farm buildings line the approach to the river, and near the crossroads on the main road is a small, early nineteenth-century school bearing the arms of the Harpur-Crewes, a pretty little building now becoming derelict. Close to the lane leading to Stenson is a fragment of the old hall, now a farmhouse. Grand views upstream to Willington Power Station.

Unstone (5). Close to Dronfield: dormitory area for Sheffield and Chesterfield. Church built 1920.

Walton-on-Trent (17). A Bailey bridge crosses the Trent here; to the N the giant cooling towers and chimneys of Drakelowe Power Station are not far away—they are an all-pervading presence in this part of the county. Interesting mediaeval church. Perp. W tower. Norman S arcade. An interior scraped, but adorned by the highly decorative rood screen and other carvings by a previous incumbent. Monuments to Disbrowe family under the tower, and to Thomas Bearcroft, a former rector (1680) in chancel. Modern stained glass by Christopher Webb.

Walton Hall stands on high ground to the S overlooking the river: a tall, handsome early eighteenth-century brick house, with top parapet and giant pilasters, built for the Disbrowes. Cheerful stuccoed rectory opposite the church, with faint Gothick decoration.

Wardlow (5). Main-road hamlet in spectacular country near Tideswell. Small Victorian Perp. church of 1873.

Wessington (8). Small village round a large gorse-strewn green on the high ground between Matlock and Alfreton. Little turreted church of 1859.

Weston-on-Trent (15). The church stands in a field some little way to

◁ Wingfield Manor,
SOUTH WINGFIELD

the W of the village, and is prettily situated with views over the river to the ancient oaks of Donington Park, across in Leicestershire. Perp. spire. Very wide nave with lofty arcades, and a single gable roof over nave and aisles together. Monument in S aisle to Richard Sale (d. 1615): kneeling figures and other fragments recently restored by descendants, and lurid figure of skeleton with pick and shovel and the Latin inscription: "Ecce nosce te ipsum. Ut sum, tu eris". Also monument in chancel to Richard Sale, Prebendary of Lichfield and Rector 1625. Attractive tiles in sanctuary.

A gate by the lane to the church bears the unexpected notice: "To Ukrainian Youth Camp".

Whaley Bridge (4). In the Peak country between Buxton and New Mills. Small industrial town which grew up in the nineteenth century with the arrival of the railway. Near the station is the Jodrell Arms (early nineteenth century); Holy Trinity, Fernilee, was built in 1904, and the chancel added in 1922—a pretty art nouveau building. This part of the county has the ecclesiastical distinction of being in the Diocese of Chester, and Taxal is the mother parish. Fernilee Reservoir was formed from the flooded Goyt valley after the first world war.

Whitwell (6) in the coal country of NE Derbyshire, but the village is largely unspoilt. It is dominated by a church of unusual size and splendour. Grand Norman nave with clerestory, great Norman chancel arch, admired by Temple Moore as "one of the most perfect, if not the most perfect Norman arch" he had ever seen; Decorated chancel and transepts with beautiful traceried windows, sedilia and Easter Sepulchre. Tomb to Sir Roger Manners (son of Dorothy Vernon of Haddon), 1632. Rectory by J. L. Pearson, and manor house (seventeenth century) complete a most satisfying group.

Willington (14). The village was cut in half by the railway embankment in the nineteenth century, and has been overwhelmed by the vast powerstation in this. It has changed not only the character but the scale of

everything here. The little church is an unassuming building, chiefly of the early nineteenth century. A Norman tympanum survives from previous building. Most of the interior is in keeping with the date of 1824: plastered ceiling, cast-iron altar rails, eighteenth-century font. Views across the Trent to Repton.

Wilne (15). Lost in the water meadows close to where the Derwent joins the Trent is the grand church of Wilne. Over the centuries floods have apparently driven the population up to *Draycott* (which is a western extension of Breaston); only the church, an old mill and two pairs of cottages survive. Exterior distinguished and embattled; interior spacious and beautifully refurnished after a fire of 1917. Saxon font, one of the oldest in England. Handsome Arts-and-Crafts-inspired rood screen and other furnishings. Of special interest is the Willoughby chapel, on S side of the chancel, undamaged by the fire. Built in 1622 for the Willoughbys of Risley (q.v.), for whom Wilne was then the parish church. Like Risley church, this is a case of Gothic survival; in fact this is the more remarkable, as it is thirty years later, and could easily have been built a hundred years earlier. Notable and beautiful seventeenth-century continental stained glass—three windows which immediately take you from Trentside to Bruges. Great, but conventional, tomb of Sir John Willoughby (d. 1622), with recumbent effigies. Much less conventional the large pedestal monument crowned with noble urn with supporting cherubs, charmingly baroque, in memory of Ann Willoughby, wife of the Hon. Anchitel Grey (d. 1688). Rarest and most charming of all—for an English church—the gay seventeenth-century continental tiles on the floor. Small earlier brasses to the family too.

Wingerworth (8). Chesterfield stretches out with its long tentacles of villas and bungalows, and the old village is now sadly suburbanised. A great new church has been built on to the N side of the ancient building. The plan is ingenious, as the old nave forms a narthex to the new church, which is orientated to the N,

121

and the Norman arcade, with the clerestory above, is opened up, framing the view into the new building. The old church contains a rare mediaeval rood loft, a thirteenth-century effigy of a priest, and many memorials to the old recusant family of Hunloke. These are chiefly in the form of ledger stones in the sanctuary, but to the N side of the chancel (approached from the outside) is the eighteenth-century mausoleum of the family. Wingerworth Hall was built for Sir Thomas Hunloke, 3rd Bt, in 1729, by Francis Smith of Warwick, but was pulled down between the wars, and only the two side wings remain, to the SE of the church. The 1st Bt was knighted by Charles I on the battlefield of Edge Hill.

North Wingfield (9). An imposing church, set in a fine position in this rather drab countryside: grand Perp. W tower, spacious nave, lofty cle-restoried chancel, vaulted S porch. Most of this is fourteenth–fifteenth century, but there is an interesting Norman window at the E end of the N aisle, opening into the chantry beyond. Thirteenth-century effigy of a knight (perhaps Sir John Deincourt) in chancel recess, defaced mediaeval sculptures in S aisle and chantry, seventeenth-century font, ancient wooden S door, modern rood screen, repainted Royal Arms of Elizabeth I. Monuments in chantry to Holland family, of Ford House; one with medallion portrait to "John Holland Esquire of Ford in the County of Derby, which villa it was his amusement to adorn with valuable paintings, the works of his own pencil; while those who loved this truly hospitable man, amongst whom were numbered a Wright, a Mason and a Gray, saw portrayed. . . ." etc. John Holland was an attractive personality, a great friend of Wright of Derby, and his house the centre of a gay, artistic, literary circle; he is mentioned a good deal in Benedict Nicolson's book on Joseph Wright (1969). Ford was a pleasant Georgian mansion, demolished in 1958. Near the S door is a recoloured monument to John Brailsford; it is dated 1714, but is of strongly seventeenth-century character. Distinguished Georgian rectory at E end of church, with a mean modern house built in front.

South Wingfield (11). A dull village in the Amber valley, and close to industry. But set on the higher ground to the S is the wonderful and enormous mediaeval pile of Wingfield Manor. In date and in character it is a second Haddon Hall—but in ruins.

An unpromising farm road leads up to the place, which is the private property of the farmer who lives there. Here is none of the ordered tidiness of a Ministry of Works ancient monument, but the un-sophisticated beauty of a slightly overgrown ruin. The house consists of two quadrangles and is approached by a muddy cow-yard; barns and out-buildings flank the arched entrance gateway, and to the right of the gateway itself a modern farmhouse has been contrived in the ancient shell. Here it is possible to buy a guidebook and pay the entrance fee.

The inner quadrangle is dominated by an ancient leaning walnut tree; the centre is occupied by a kitchen garden, and across the cabbages and runner beans is the great S façade of the house itself. To the right of the porch is the Great Hall; to the left the high gable and traceried window of the State Apartments. On the W side (behind the walnut) was the suite of rooms occupied by Mary Queen of Scots in 1569 and 1584. The SW corner is occupied by the great High Tower (72 ft). Finest of all, under the Hall, is a magnificent vaulted undercroft.

The house was built in the middle of the fifteenth century by Ralph Lord Cromwell, who subsequently sold it to the 2nd Earl of Shrewsbury. It was the 6th Earl (who married Bess of Hardwick) who accommodated Mary Queen of Scots here. It was twice captured in the Civil War, and dismantled in 1646. After a complicated succession the place was bought in 1666 by Immanuel Halton, a distinguished mathematician, and he converted the Great Hall into a two-storeyed house. His grandson dismantled more of the house to build the square Wingfield Hall down the hill in 1774. The house is delight-fully surrounded by farmland and orchards; it is possible to climb at will among the ruins.

The church, too, stands apart from the village and near the railway. It is in origin a mediaeval building, but was done up in Georgian times. Halton monument in chancel.

Another notable building is S Wingfield Station, "the most perfect of all station houses", according to Christian Barman. The line was engineered by Stephenson and opened in 1840. The architect of the station was Francis Thompson.

Winster (8). Old lead-mining town, close to grand Peakland scenery. Several handsome eighteenth-century houses, notably the Hall, with its giant pilasters and balustraded top; and Stanley House with its Venetian windows. The Market House belongs to the National Trust. The upper floor is of brick, and seventeenth century, with mullioned windows; but the ground floor is of stone and mediaeval, with pointed arches which were originally open. The church is strange, with double nave (of 1842) divided by lofty arcade, and W tower of 1721. Fine tombs in churchyard.

Wirksworth (11). An ancient, slightly faded little town of much atmosphere —faded because its great days as the centre of the old lead-mining industry are over, and several streets and houses have a threadbare beauty about them. The church is in its own little enclosure, a little close or churchyard entered from the surrounding streets by mysterious alleys with old gate-piers. Footpaths encircle it; on the N side is the eighteenth-century Vicarage; the Grammar School, founded by Anthony Gell in 1584 and rebuilt in pretty pinnacled Perp. style in 1828, and Gell's Almshouses (1584) are at the E end.

Wonderful cruciform church, partly early English, partly Dec. partly Perp. Nave, lower part of central tower, and long-aisled chancel are thirteenth century; the tower was heightened in the fourteenth, and the clerestory and embattled and pin-nacled exterior belong to the fifteenth. Interior of many vistas. Interesting monuments to Gell family of Hopton including Anthony Gell,

YOULGREAVE ▷

founder of the school, the celebrated Sir John Gell, Parliamentary General and 1st Bt, and Sir Philip Gell, 3rd and last Bt, who married a Fagge of Wiston in Sussex. Two fonts, one Norman, one seventeenth century. Royal Arms of William IV. But most important is the ninth-century Anglo-Saxon coffin lid, dug up in the chancel, face downwards, in 1820. This is set in the N aisle wall. It is evidently part of a tomb, perhaps of an early missionary. The scenes depict episodes in the life of Christ, such as the raising of Jairus' daughter, the washing of the disciples' feet, the burial and the ascension. There are also many Norman fragments in the N transept.

In Chapel Lane is the Moot Hall (a rebuilding of 1814), where the Barmote Courts are held. Preserved here is the great bronze Miners' Standard Dish (temp. Henry VIII) for measuring the lead. Wirksworth is a town of steep hills, narrow terraces and many old houses; suffice here to mention the Red Lion facing the Market Place, the fine eighteenth-century stone house next door; and, opposite, the delightful, undisturbed old shop-front of Payne the Chemist.

Woodville (17). Part of the mining sprawl of Swadlincote; there is one little back alley marked The City, and another gloomy street called Sun Street. The church is by Stevens (1846) in his Norman style; attractive atmospheric interior, wide, lofty, well furnished.

Wormhill (4). Secret village, close to Miller's Dale. From the road it is possible to look down through two pairs of gate-piers to the Hall, an attractive seventeenth-century stone house, built (and still owned) by the Bagshawe family. Mullioned windows. Segmental, pedimented front door approached by flight of steps. The church was rebuilt in 1864 and is full of handsome Victorian furnishings and hatchments. W tower, of which the base is ancient, has a Rhenish cap, like Sompting.

Yeaveley (11). Small brick church built in 1840, with a little embattled brick tower. The architect was J. Smith. A mile to the W, deeply hidden in a remote valley, and a mile from the main road by a muddy private lane, stand the remains of Stydd Hall, formerly a Preceptory of the Knights Hospitaller. One wall of the chapel survives, with a few thirteenth-century lancet windows. Alongside is a tall, square, brick Elizabethan house, now a farmhouse, but embellished in the early nineteenth century with Strawberry Hill Gothick bay windows. A remote and altogether mysterious place.

Youlgreave (8). High up in the grand country between Ashbourne and Bakewell; a big village, dominated by its great church. Tall Perp. tower— all the church appears externally Perp., with its battlements and pinnacles. Spacious interior—wide aisles and, surprisingly, a Norman arcade. This was later extended to the W, without aisles, to connect with the new Perp. tower, and the whole was crowned with its clerestory, and its roof. Chancel of some splendour, with the elegant little late-fifteenth-century tomb of Thomas Cockayne in its centre, and E window and S window by Burne-Jones. Norman Shaw restored the church in 1870, and there are further nineteenth-century windows by Kempe. The thirteenth-century font is unique—with its separate projecting side bowl. Further monuments of interest, notably the alabaster panel in N aisle to Robert Gilbert, showing him and his wife and their seventeen children grouped round the Virgin (1492).

To the W of the village, and a mile off the Ashbourne–Buxton road, is the most famous of the Derbyshire Stone Circles, Arbor Low. It is 250 ft in diameter, surrounded by a ditch, and protected by a bank 6 ft high, and has two entrances, opposite each other. There are forty-six great stones, lying down and pointing inwards towards the central sanctuary. It belongs to the late Stone Age or early Bronze Age (c. 2000 B.C.), and is connected with the various large barrows in the vicinity. The lane leading to it is called Long Rake.

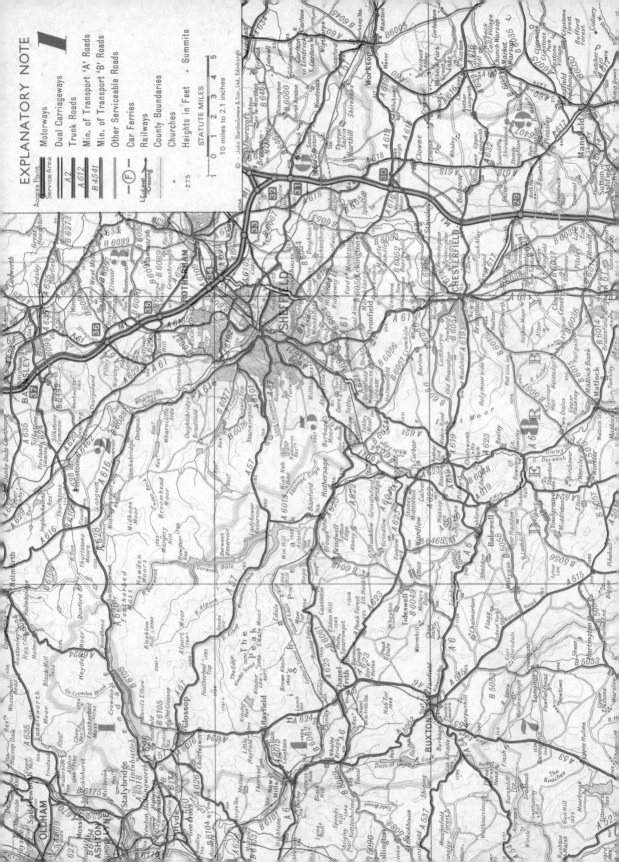

EXPLANATORY NOTE

Access Point
Service Area
Motorways
Dual Carriageways
A2 Trunk Roads
A612 Min. of Transport 'A' Roads
B 4541 Min. of Transport 'B' Roads
Other Serviceable Roads
Car Ferries
Railways
County Boundaries
Churches
Heights in Feet   Summits
·275

STATUTE MILES
1 0 1 2 3 4 5
10 miles to 2.1 inches

Level
Crossing

Index